, ..., a priest in Church of England with more ... years experience of training Readers. Until early 2009, she was Director of Reader Studies and Diocesan Director of Ordinands in York Diocese. Cathy is now the Principal of 'Lindisfarne', the Church of England's Regional Training Partnership in north-east England.

Paula Gooder was a lecturer in Biblical Studies at Ripon College Cuddesdon and then at the Queen's Foundation for Ecumenical Theological Studies for a total of 12 years before beginning to work freelance as a writer and lecturer in biblical studies. She is a visiting lecturer at King's College London, an honorary lecturer at the University of Birmingham, a research scholar at the Queen's Foundation, Birmingham, a Reader in the Diocese of Birmingham and Canon Theologian of Birmingham Cathedral. A published author, her previous books include *Exploring New Testament Greek: A Way In* (co-authored with Peter Kevern, SCM Press, 2004), *Only the Third Heaven? 2 Corinthians 12.1–10 and Heavenly Ascent* (T&T Clark, 2006), *Searching for Meaning: An Introduction to Interpreting the New Testament* (SPCK, 2008) and *The Meaning is in the Waiting: The Spirit of Advent* (Canterbury Press, 2008).

# READER MINISTRY EXPLORED

CATHY ROWLING
and
PAULA GOODER

First published in Great Britain in 2009

Society for Promoting Christian Knowledge
36 Causton Street
London SW1P 4ST

The author and publisher have made every effort to ensure that the
external website and email addresses included in this book are correct
and up to date at the time of going to press. The author and publisher
are not responsible for the content, quality or continuing accessibility
of the sites.

*British Library Cataloguing-in-Publication Data*
A catalogue record for this book is available from the British Library

ISBN 978–0–281–05981–2
1 3 5 7 9 10 8 6 4 2

Typeset by Graphicraft Ltd, Hong Kong
Printed in Great Britain by Ashford Colour Press

Produced on paper from sustainable forests

# Contents

Contents

# Foreword

'There are varieties of gifts, but the same Spirit; and there are varieties of service, but the same Lord; and there are varieties of working, but it is the same God who inspires them all in every one.' These words from St Paul's first letter to the Corinthians bring a message of inspiration and energy. God calls his people, now as then, to serve him and to be his witnesses in his world. He calls many people to teach and preach in his name. And in the Anglican Church we are blessed by having a strong ministry of Readers who do just that.

This is a book for people who are concerned in any way with Reader ministry. Whether you are a potential Reader, someone in training or already licensed, the colleague or tutor of a Reader or involved in planning the future of Reader ministry more widely, there will be much in this book to excite you, and to help to shape your thinking, your prayers and your work.

During the whole of her public ministry, Cathy Rowling has worked with Readers and candidates for Reader ministry. This book comes out of a huge amount of experience, and from deep reflection about what Reader ministry is and what it could be. As well as being a biblical scholar of international standing, Paula Gooder brings the first-hand insights of being a Reader. I am grateful to them both for working together and for producing this valuable resource.

*Sentamu Ebor:*
*Archbishop of York*

# Acknowledgements

We owe a great debt of gratitude to Paul Ferguson, Archdeacon of Cleveland and Warden of Readers in York Diocese, who read through the whole manuscript and suggested some major and a great many minor improvements to the text. Thank you too to those many Readers – in particular, but not exclusively, the Readers of York Diocese – who have been so unfailingly enthusiastic in their support of this project and so generous in sharing their stories; such thanks are due in equal measure to those whose stories appear here and to those whose contributions have helped to form and shape the book but whose names do not appear in print.

We would both like to thank our families for their support and encouragement of our writing and our ministries.

# Introduction

The question that is perhaps most frequently asked of those who have been admitted to the office of Reader and licensed to a Reader ministry in the Church of England is: 'If you're a Reader does that mean that you read in church?' Well, it quite probably does, but lots of other people do that too. While a little coaching might work wonders, people do not generally need up to three years of training to be able to stand up in church and read from the Bible. So being a Reader has to be about much more than this.[1]

Let's look again at the word 'read' to establish what this 'much more' might mean. In one sense, of course, it's perfectly true to say that part of the Reader's task is to read scripture, both publicly in church and elsewhere. The ministry of Readers was described by the House of Bishops in 1998 as being a teaching and preaching ministry in a pastoral context, and if the Church is to preach and teach effectively it needs people who have read and studied the scriptures and learnt to handle the tools of biblical enquiry, people who can draw upon the wisdom of biblical scholarship and help make sense of the Bible for today.

But as well as reading scripture the Church requires its ministers to 'read' in a wider sense. They are to read theology – and this means much more than simply reading books about God and God's engagement with the world, important as these may be. It means 'reading the things of God', perhaps (though this might sound rather a large claim to make) in much the same way as the prophets did. It is, in other words, about helping people understand and make sense of the way things are in the light of what we perceive to be God's ways. The call to ministry, then, is a call to look outwards, to proclaim the good news of Jesus Christ through words and actions that help people to make sense of the varied contexts of their daily lives; it is a call to take seriously the very real questions that people have about meaning and purpose and their own personal, spiritual quests.

Readers can be ideally placed to undertake these various forms of 'reading' with, for and on behalf of the Church:

- they have engaged in a significant amount of study before being admitted to the office of Reader and they will continue to study in ways appropriate to their gifts and relevant to the context in which they minister;
- they will have shown themselves to be men and women who have a committed, developing and maturing relationship with God through Christ;
- they are actively engaged both in the Church and, through their daily lives, in the wider world;
- they can be an effective 'bridge' between Church and world and between world and Church;
- they can 'read' contemporary society, both in local communities and with regard to the bigger issues of the day;
- they are those, in other words, who can 'read between the lines', looking at what is *and isn't* overtly stated; discerning, interpreting and presenting the words and ways of God, and clothing them with real, contextualized meaning.

Readers are a vital part of the life of the Church and its ministry. In purely practical terms the Church of England could not function week by week without its Readers. The public ministry of the Church currently comprises some 27,000 licensed ministers: about 9,000 paid clergy; just over 2,000 non-stipendiary ministers; approximately 5,000 active retired clergy; 1,100 chaplains in colleges, universities, hospitals, schools, prisons and the armed forces; and more than 10,000 Readers. It is hardly surprising, then, that in many parishes and benefices it is Readers who make the local pattern of worship sustainable Sunday by Sunday and who undertake a significant amount of the day-to-day ministry in a parish during the week. This is likely to be particularly true of rural areas where there might be ten or more churches in a benefice that serves a group of small, scattered communities.

In addition to the enhanced engagement of Readers in the world as outlined above, Readers' involvement in the parish includes such things as:

- leading non-sacramental worship, which might include Morning and Evening Prayer, services of the word, all-age worship and, increasingly, the conduct of funerals;
- preaching in a wide variety of contexts;

- teaching or leading groups, for example Bible study groups, baptism preparation meetings and confirmation classes;
- taking Holy Communion to people who are in nursing homes or who are housebound;
- visiting people in hospital;
- and a wide range of other pastoral work as is needed in the place in which they minister.

While most Readers are involved in leading worship and in parish activities such as these, for many it will be the workplace in which their Reader ministry is lived out day by day. This will be explored more fully in a later chapter, but for now, read what Christine, a retail manager, said when asked how being a Reader had made an impact upon her working life:

> People know what I do and what I stand for. They expect me to speak out and they know that I'm not afraid of saying when I think something is wrong. I don't push God at my colleagues but they will often ask me to pray for someone or some situation. I usually say, 'Of course I will, but why don't you pray yourself – or better still, let's pray together.'

Such a response sits well alongside words from the foreword to *Bridging the Gap*: 'Here is a trained, authorized ministry freely given in order that the message of the gospel can be better understood and people helped and encouraged by those who live and work alongside them' (Kuhrt and Nappin (eds), 2002, p. vii).

Reader ministry is relevant to every part of life: *Reader Ministry Explored* looks at what it might mean to be called to Reader ministry, where that ministry sits within the whole spectrum of the Church's wider ministry, what is likely to be involved in selection and in the different areas of training, and how people exercise Reader ministry in a variety of contexts.

It is likely to be most helpful for those beginning to explore their sense of a call to Reader ministry but will also be valuable for those who have already been licensed but who want to reflect more deeply about what their calling to Reader ministry entails. Much of the book is focused on practical issues such as public ministry, selection, training and the nature of Reader ministry in the Church as a whole. It may seem odd that walking with God, through intercession, contemplative prayer and the devotional reading of scripture is not much mentioned in the book. This is not because we consider it to be unimportant but because it is so important that we see it as underpinning everything else. Your own devotional life flows out of your relationship with God and into everything that you do. Reader ministry – like all other ministries in the Church – is predicated upon your relationship with God. Without that relationship, your ministry has no roots.

*Reader Ministry Explored* is written as a practical guide for candidates, trainees and licensed Readers and it is offered to the Church as a contribution to the ongoing discussion that is taking place at every level of church life about the role and nature of its authorized ministry. The book is split into three main sections.

- The first section explores what public ministry is and where Reader ministry came from.
- The second section focuses on the questions that might be raised by those who are considering whether it might be right to offer themselves for Reader ministry; it looks at discernment of vocation, selection and training.
- The final, third, section examines Reader ministry in the Church today and gives examples of some of the different expressions of Reader ministry that you might want to consider.

Some people will find the whole book helpful; others will concentrate on particular sections of it. This is fine; the chapters are designed to follow on one from another but also to make sense independently of the rest of the book.

Finally a personal note. As authors of this book we both have a longstanding involvement in Reader ministry: Cathy as someone who trained Readers in York Diocese for many years until early 2009 and who now works in theological education in the North East, and Paula as a Reader in the Birmingham Diocese. We are both, in our different ways, passionate about the contribution that Readers make to the public ministry of the Church of England and hope, in your reading of this book, that you will share with us in celebrating what Readers already do in the Church and in dreaming dreams of what Reader ministry might be in the years to come.

# Part 1

# UNDERSTANDING READER MINISTRY

# 1

# Public ministry as a part of the ministry of the whole people of God

## Introduction

For many people when they first attend a church, and in fact for many years after that as well, ministry is something that someone else does. You may have had the experience yourself of looking at the people involved in the life and work of your church and admiring what they do without any feeling at all that you should join in. Over time, however, people are drawn into the life of a church and begin to want to make a contribution, whether it be in simple ways like talking to people or making the tea, or in more obvious ways like leading the intercessions and preaching. People are often surprised when it is pointed out that what they are doing is ministry, because they usually associate that with the clergy and a few extra 'special' people who help them. Nevertheless, the ministries of a wide range of people are essential for the health and vitality of all our churches.

If we were to rely on just a few people in ministry then our churches would do fewer and fewer things, and those in 'ministry' would run themselves ragged trying to keep even those few things going.

This chapter will explore what ministry is in general before looking at specifically public ministry in the Church of England.

## What is ministry?

Ministry is one of those words that is notoriously hard to define. In many dictionaries the definition of ministry as being what a professional minister does as part of his or her duties appears before the more general definition of it being simply the act of 'ministering'. It is no wonder, then, that so many people assume that ministry is connected with what a paid 'minister' does. In fact this is only a small part of what ministry is. In order to understand ministry it can be helpful to go back to the time of Jesus and the earliest Christian communities to see how the idea of ministry began to develop.

## On being a disciple . . .

One of the very first things that Jesus did as a part of his own ministry was to call people to follow him. In Matthew and Mark, immediately after Jesus came out of the wilderness after his temptations, Jesus called people to follow him (Matt. 4.18–22; Mark 1.17–20); it is marginally later in Luke (5.1–11; after Jesus' reading of the scriptures in the synagogue 4.16–44), but still at the start of his ministry. One of the first things that Jesus does, then, is to call people to follow him. The Gospels recount that very soon there is a company of people described as Jesus' disciples (Mark 2.15). Of course a disciple is someone who heard and hears Jesus' call, gets up and follows, but there is more to being a disciple than mere following. The Greek word for disciple is *mathētēs*, which, like the Latin word *discipulus* from which we get the word disciple, means a learner. Like those people who walked and talked with Jesus, we don't follow him in the sense of simply trailing around after him; we follow Jesus so that we can become learners of Jesus, being inspired by him, his words and deeds. Jesus' disciples, like the disciples of many other rabbis at the same time (and, we might conclude from the Gospels, John the Baptist), learnt from him largely by spending time with him, listening to him, asking questions and observing what he did. Although Jesus did 'teach' them with sayings, commands and stories, it was the time they spent with him getting things wrong, asking stupid questions and generally just being with him that transformed them bit by bit.

It wasn't long, however, before Jesus began to send out his disciples to proclaim. Indeed Mark tells us that this was in fact why he called them in the first place: 'And he appointed twelve whom he also named apostles [meaning envoys, 'those who are sent'], to be with him, and to be sent out to proclaim the message, and to have authority to cast out demons' (Mark 3.14–15). They were not just to be with Jesus but were also to go out to do the work he gave them. Later on he sent out the twelve (Matt. 10.5–14; Mark 6.7–13; Luke 9.1–6) and also a larger group of 70 (Luke 10.1–11) to proclaim the gospel, heal the sick and cast out demons. It is worth noticing that Jesus didn't wait until the disciples knew everything before he sent them out. They went out while they were still getting lots of things wrong and misunderstanding who Jesus was. We do not have to wait to be 'perfect' disciples before Jesus will ask us to do anything; in the midst of our imperfections, uncertainties and anxiety Jesus still sends us out. If we wait until we have really 'got it' before we go, we may be waiting a very long time indeed.

## On ministry . . .

It is quite common these days to make a distinction between 'being' and 'doing' – in our frenetic, busy world we have become 'professional doers' and struggle just to 'be'. Some people helpfully point out that we are 'human beings' and not 'human doings' and so we should spend more time simply 'being' and less time running around madly. At first glance this distinction maps onto the difference between discipleship and ministry: discipleship is the place where we learn to 'be' in the presence of Jesus and ministry is our 'doing' on behalf of Christ. Of course, as with many things, this distinction can be drawn too sharply. We do need to spend time just 'being', but 'being' without 'doing' makes us saggy and lazy; just as 'doing' without 'being' makes us frenetic, anxious and over-busy. Equally, discipleship is not just about 'being': it also involves doing, following, listening, learning and being sent out by Jesus; nor is ministry just about doing – being alongside others is a vital part of ministry. Jesus calls us, then, to a life of being that flows into doing, and doing informed by being.

So, how does ministry relate to discipleship? In order to address this question we need to acknowledge that this is not a question the New Testament seeks to ask or to answer. The earliest Christian communities did not attempt to sit down and define discipleship, ministry or indeed office in the Church. All we can do is to look at what they did say and attempt to draw some insights for our own lives. Part of the problem is the fact that the earliest Christians used an everyday word for what we now call ministry. The Greek word *diakonia*, which our English versions often translate as 'ministry', was often used simply to describe what servants (in Greek *diakonoi*) do. In the New Testament we can find this word used to describe people who were actually servants (e.g. in John 2.9 it is used to describe the servants who drew the water for Jesus to turn into

wine); the role of people who weren't servants but who expressed
humility through service (e.g. Jesus uses it of himself in Mark 10.45
to say that he came not to serve but to be served; and Paul uses
it of Epaphras in Col. 1.7); but also of people who had a specific
function in the Church (e.g. 1 Tim. 3.8 gives a description of what
*diakonoi* or deacons must do). Our challenge, then, is to try and
work out what this word meant to the earliest Christians and why
it became so important to describe what Christians do.

The Greek words that are often translated 'ministry' and 'minister'
can also be translated 'service' and 'servant'. This is a helpful place to
start defining ministry: just as Jesus saw himself as a humble servant
of the whole world so we are called to follow in his footsteps and
serve others too, putting their needs above our own and caring for
them. This is not all that ministry is about, however. Servants serve
masters, and are sent about their business by those to whom they
owe allegiance. In the same kind of way, ministry is not just 'social
work': we are called by God, sent out into the world to serve as Jesus
served us. It is these two aspects, loving service and commissioned
agency, that give a shape and form to the concept of ministry.

People sometimes discuss who should minister, that is, just a
few or the whole people of God. Even though the New Testament
does give us a picture of emerging roles in the Church, it may well
be that the earliest Christians might have greeted such a question
with blank bemusement. This is because of a slight confusion among
modern-day Christians about the nature of ministry. Often in the
Church we confuse 'ministry' with 'public ministry': in other words,
ministry is assumed to be standing at the front in church, leading
worship, preaching and so on. This is only one small aspect of ministry: Jesus called everyone to care for each other, to go out into the
world proclaiming the gospel, to be a Christian in the place in which
they live. In this sense we are all called to be ministers, or servants
of God, joining in with God's mission to the world.

'Public ministry' is a term that is used to describe a particular
aspect of ministry within the shared life of the witnessing, serving,
caring Church. Although Paul is very clear in 1 Corinthians 12 and
Romans 12 that everyone in the Body of Christ was to use the gifts
that God had given them and that all gifts were to be equally
valued in the Body (and incidentally this is a lesson that still needs

to be learned fully within our churches where some gifts are still regarded as more important than others), this was not intended to mean that everyone did everything. As time went on in the earliest Christian communities, we find evidence that the communities did begin to identify 'offices', that is, specific roles which were more clearly tied to 'public ministry' than the care of the Body of Christ for its members and the world in general. If you are exploring Reader ministry (or indeed are a Reader already) then it is the more public aspect of ministry to which you feel called.

## Public ministry within the Church

Public ministry differs from ministry in general because it carries with it the recognition and authority of the Church. Those who are involved in public ministry, to a certain extent, represent the Church and so are accountable to it. This does not imply that they are more important than others within the Church, but they do have a greater burden of responsibility. Consequently, all authorized ministry carries a licence to minister, issued under the bishop's authority, and the licence does two things: it gives permission and it makes people accountable. These are opposite sides of the same coin. If people are speaking of Christ in the Church's name, it is good for others to know that they have the authority of the Church to do so. People should be able to trust that anyone whom the Church licenses as a Reader has been appropriately assessed to ensure that they have met standards relating to their personal integrity and adherence to the Church's understanding of the Christian faith, and that they have been appropriately trained.

Sometimes people say that they want a 'free-floating' Reader ministry that isn't rooted in the life of a particular church community but that leaves them free simply to engage in whatever ministerial opportunities present themselves here and there. But context is important and in order for people to exercise a public ministry in the Church of England they must be authorized to minister in a particular place by their diocesan bishop, either in the form of a licence to a particular benefice or chaplaincy, or, if over the age of 70 (and sometimes for other reasons), in the form of Permission to Officiate.

In a similar way, all public ministry needs to have the backing of the wider Church; someone can't become a Reader simply because their congregation thinks it would be a good idea. While the views of the parish and its incumbent will play an important part in the process of selection, the perspective of the Church beyond the parish will also be sought, so a candidate will be asked to meet with those experienced in ministry – including one or more Readers – and this in turn may lead to interviews with people who represent the Church more widely, perhaps at deanery or diocesan level. This process is an important one, for it reflects the fact that the Church is much bigger than any one individual's immediate situation. When they have finished training, Reader candidates are admitted to the office of Reader in the Church of God and they are separately, though usually at the same service, given a licence to a particular sphere of ministry. This means that they undertake to work collaboratively with their vicar, rural dean or chaplain who, in turn, will nurture their ministry and support them. Importantly, this emphasis on the ministry of the whole Church rather than simply of a particular local context, expressed through national standards of selection and training, means that if someone moves to a new parish or diocese their Reader ministry can be transferred. They will be given a new licence to minister in their new context but they are not admitted into the office of Reader in the Church of God again – that only happens once.

So the Church places great responsibility on those whom it authorizes to its public ministry, and responsibility brings in turn added accountability. The New Testament encourages all Christians to be accountable to one another. The apostle Paul regularly uses the image of the Body of Christ (1 Cor. 12 and Rom. 12, as well as elsewhere) to show that all members of the Christian community, while being different from each other, depend upon each other for mutual support and accountability. This seems particularly true of the leaders in the early Church and much of 2 Corinthians concerns Paul's own 'account' of who he is and why he acts in the way that he does. This demonstrates that, intemperate though he may be in his defence of himself, he acknowledges the need to be accountable to the others in his community. This need for accountability is especially true for those who are given the Church's authority to preach and teach and lead.

Reader ministry is part of the way in which the Church of England orders its life. When the Church authorizes people as public ministers it does so within a particular framework of what it means for the Church to carry out its responsibility to proclaim the word of God. This means that all ministry has parameters. When anyone belongs to a church they are aligning themselves with its beliefs and traditions. For those who worship in an Anglican context the spectrum of accepted ways of understanding and interpreting the Christian faith is broad. But the parameters don't stretch infinitely; there comes a point beyond which things cease to be recognizably Anglican. Those who are called to a particular ministry, such as that of Reader, have a responsibility to ensure that they exercise that ministry in ways that are in line with the Church's teaching. Reference will be made later to the Canons of the Church of England, but it is worth noting here that before anyone is admitted to the office of Reader and given a licence to minister, they must make certain declarations, which, in a Church of England context, include these words:

> I (*name*) do so affirm, and accordingly declare my belief in the faith which is revealed in the Holy Scriptures and set forth in the catholic creeds and to which the historic formularies of the Church of England bear witness; and in public prayer I will use only the forms of service which are authorized or allowed by Canon.
> I (*name*) will give due obedience to the Lord Bishop of (*diocese*) and his successors in all things lawful and honest.

This makes clear the two-way nature of the Church's authentication of an individual's call. Readers are given permission to speak on behalf of the Church, but they are also obliged to abide by its teachings and to accept its authority. The need to ensure that this is thoroughly explored and understood – by the potential Reader as well as by others – explains why the process of nomination, selection and training that precedes the actual admission of the candidate to the office of Reader can sometimes appear to be a long one. Critically, when a person is admitted to the Church's public ministry, and however much that event represents the goal of the person's aspirations and hopes, it is not to be understood in terms of personal achievement and the fulfilment of ambition. In other words ministry, and the opportunity to exercise it, exists for the sake of other people, and not the minister. Ministry is the Church's expression of the fact that the good news of salvation is worth sharing with our hungry and hurting world, and it's the Church's assertion that it considers it to be worthwhile investing in the training of the few in order that the many might hear and see and know more clearly. So ministry can never just be about the individual.

We can see, then, that all ministry is both everything and nothing:

- It is everything because the Church gives us authority to speak in its name.
- It is nothing because we are the messengers and not the message.
- It is everything because we offer the whole of our lives, in all their ordinariness, to be transformed into lives that can be publicly useful for God's purposes.
- It is nothing because at the very deepest level of our being we know that it is our baptism, not our public ministry in itself, that roots and grounds us in Christ (Rom. 6.3) and enables us to speak of God.
- It is everything because we are unique, loved, forgiven, children of God, held in God's loving embrace.
- It is nothing because we are all too aware of our shortcomings and our inadequacies and our almost infinite 'smallness' within the master plan of God's love.

## Varieties of lay ministry in the Church of England

As you might expect there is a wide range of ministries within the Church, from the most informal to the most formal, from the least publicly recognized to the most prominent, authorized and licensed. As a Church we are increasingly learning to recognize and draw out the ministries of a wide range of people. This is enriching, deepening and inspiring the life of churches across the country.

The reasons for this shift are multi-layered. In many places, burgeoning lay ministry is due to the fact that people are increasingly having their eyes opened to how important it is for the life and well-being of the Church. We would fool ourselves, however, if we did not also recognize practical motivations behind it. Two factors in particular seem to be important:

- The number of clergy is decreasing and parishes and benefices have, in many parts of the country, been formed into bigger groups with fewer clergy.
- In many places money to support stipendiary ministry is tight; even if the supply of those offering for stipendiary ministry were endless, the Church of England could not afford to pay as many as it might ideally like.

But good consequences can result from changed situations and one positive aspect of this is that dioceses have been led to look afresh at their resources, both material and human. This in turn is leading to the development of new lay ministries within the Church, and to a greater recognition of the existence of others. The gifts of many lay people are being released in a new way and the demarcation between the roles of clergy and laity is being reshaped and redefined with a greater emphasis on collaboration. A cynic might be tempted to note that it appears that the Church is only putting an emphasis on the ministry of lay people because it doesn't have enough clergy to go round. Whether or not this is true, many would want to respond that, nevertheless, the Holy Spirit is at work renewing and refreshing the Church and sometimes the best results arise out of mixed motives.

It is against this backdrop that many lay people are now undertaking training to be – among other ministries – worship leaders, evangelists, catechists and pastoral workers. In some contexts the training will be a few weeks in duration, in others it may be a course that has been accredited by a university or another award-giving body. What is important is that people are trained in a way and at a level that is appropriate to their gifts, abilities and capacity for ministry. This change in the Church's approach to ministry will have an impact not only on the training of lay people but also on clergy, who, increasingly, need to work collaboratively rather than with a 'top-down' model of church. This doesn't mean that the priest will be called upon to give up his or her proper responsibilities, but that there will be a need for them to be exercised differently. The training of clergy is now beginning to embrace the need to encourage an understanding of ministry as a shared and collaborative enterprise in which every member of the Church is encouraged to play a full part.

## Do we need Reader ministry?

One of the effects of the changing patterns of lay ministries within the Church is that Reader ministry can feel increasingly squeezed. What, some people might want to ask, is the point of a Reader if other people can lead worship, do pastoral work, take a full role in ministerial teams and even, in some circumstances, preach? The answer is complex but important. The inherent value of Reader ministry lies not in the fact that it does anything 'unique' – there is nothing that a Reader can do that cannot be done by other people in the Church either lay or ordained – but in the confluence, or flowing together, of certain characteristics.

Readers are:

- public ministers authorized nationally by the Church of England for a ministry that is transferable throughout the country;
- public ministers licensed to a local context, rooted and supported in that local context;
- lay ministers called as lay people to minister in the midst of other lay members of the Church;
- theologically trained and articulate;
- licensed to preach, teach and engage in pastoral work; to lead Morning and Evening Prayer and to administer Holy Communion; to bury the dead (with the goodwill of the family) (from Canon E4).

It is the bringing together of this range of characteristics that is unique to Reader ministry and vital for the welfare and health of the Church.

## Church Army evangelists

Readers, however, are not the only public, licensed lay ministers; Church Army evangelists are also public representative ministers of the Church of England. Church Army was founded in 1882 by Wilson Carlile, a clergyman in London, who saw that the Church was struggling to engage meaningfully with the very many poor people of the city. Church Army has a long tradition of pioneering evangelism. Its ministry is often among those who have little or no meaningful contact with either the Church or Christianity.

Our vision is to have teams working in pioneering contexts and relevant ways, reaching out to those people and communities that have had little contact with the good news, and starting up fresh expressions of church with which they can engage and develop in. Around 350 full-time lay Church Army Evangelists minister in this context. We select people who are gifted and called to work specifically with the unchurched and among those who are marginalized in our society. Church Army has its own selection process and training. Training happens on mission bases around the UK and is up to four years in length. After training, people are commissioned as Church Army Evangelists and admitted to the Office of Evangelist in the Church of England, by an archbishop or bishop at a special service each year.

(Ray Khan, Candidates' Secretary, Church Army)

The Church Army website <www.churcharmy.org.uk> is a useful source of information for those wondering what form their ministry should take. The website states the following: 'Church Army is about communicating the unchanging message of an unchanging God to a fast-changing culture and its evangelists continue to reach out and make church effective by meeting people where they are.' Church Army projects include working with the homeless, prisoners, self-harm victims, women involved in prostitution, people living on deprived housing estates, working with younger and older people, and engaging with many other areas of need. Church Army also equips and works in partnership with local churches and other organizations in rural, suburban and urban settings to develop appropriate and relevant forms of Christian community in the twenty-first century.

## Reader ministry

Let's return to Reader ministry and look at it in a little more detail. The descriptor of Reader ministry as set out by the House of Bishops in 1989 is that it is a 'Preaching and teaching ministry in a pastoral context'. While there are those in the Church at the moment who would like to see Reader ministry more closely defined, especially in the light of the many other lay ministries that have emerged and that continue to emerge, it may well be that such an approach would be counterproductive. It may simply be better to see Reader ministry as being made up of a large number of interweaving strands:

- a firm rooting within the ministry of the whole Church;
- a public, representative ministry;
- not 'status dependent';
- having an identity that sets it free from merely being the 'vicar's helper' and that is ratified by the local church community;
- nationally recognized and accredited;
- theologically equipped;
- taking seriously the question: 'How can the unity of life and service be maintained in a compartmentalized world?' (Andrew Britton in Kuhrt and Nappin, 2002);
- acknowledging that all ministry is about proclaiming 'a God of mission who has a Church not about a God of the Church which has a mission' (Dearborn, 1998).

And there are many other strands. This definition of Reader ministry is expansive and far from exhaustive but gives something of an initial flavour of the ministry that can be best identified as Reader ministry.

Reader ministry is a dynamic ministry. The constraints and parameters provided by the framework set out above would seem to be sufficient to ensure that it retains its distinctiveness among the many expressions of Christ's ongoing ministry in which all the baptized are called to share, without tighter definition. To be relevant to the Church, Reader ministry must remain open to God's leading and directing; educated, informed, contextually based, culturally aware and able to respond to contemporary need. It will give due regard to its history because this informs the present, but it won't allow itself to become encumbered by that history or fossilized at any given point in its development. The story of Reader ministry over the years is one of flexibility and adaptability – these are among the greatest gifts that it can offer the Church.

# 2

# Tracing the history of Reader ministry

We have seen that Reader ministry plays an important role in the Church's public ministry today, but this has not always been the case. This chapter will explore the story of Reader ministry. This is important because although the past does not need to dictate the way that things are done now – nor the way they might be done in the future – understanding something about the past helps us to understand the present.

## The ancient origins of Reader ministry?

### The early Church

Some accounts of the history of Reader ministry look back to origins in the earliest Christian communities. In Luke 4 we have a reference to Jesus reading in the synagogue, and elsewhere in the New Testament of people 'reading' in Christian worship (Col. 4.16; Rev. 1.3). These can be seen as little more than descriptive references. Most people would have been illiterate so it is inevitable that some must have read while others listened. This of itself does not give us sufficient grounds upon which to build a theology of Reader ministry.

Some of those who have written about Reader ministry in the past (see the list of further reading at the end of this chapter) have attempted to trace the origins of Reader ministry to the work of Justin Martyr (a Christian writer and thinker *c.* 100–*c.* 165) who describes a person who could read intelligently from scripture as a lector (*First Apology* LXVII.1). Despite this brief reference in the early second century AD to lectors, it is not really until around the year AD 200 and the writings of Tertullian that we find lectors established as part of the ministry of the Church. In some places the lector would also expound the meaning of the passage, in others they would withdraw from worship to teach those seeking baptism (Tertullian, *De Praescriptione Haereticorum* XLI.8).

There is also evidence of people who had not been ordained deacon being allowed to lead worship, to bury the dead and purify women after childbirth, though not to preach or to administer the sacraments. But the practice of the early Church appears to have varied so much from one place to another that it is difficult to be categorical about anything. Whether this liturgical ministry as exercised in the early centuries of the Church can be seen as a model for an understanding of the Reader as preacher and teacher in today's Church is open to debate. In any case, by the Middle Ages the Church had lost any real notion of the office of lector being a distinctive lay ministry with the actual function of reading at worship, and so lectors cannot be regarded as being, in any way, the direct ancestors of Reader ministry.

## The Elizabethan period

The Church of England flirted briefly with something similar to modern Reader ministry during the reign of Elizabeth I, when the Archbishop of Canterbury, Matthew Parker, created a number of Readers on account of there not being enough clergy to staff the parishes. The intention was to provide a basic level of ministry that ensured that the offices of matins and evensong were read in parishes where there were no clergy. The venture was not in any real sense intended to be an attempt at recognizing the gifts that lay people could legitimately bring to the tasks of leading the Church's worship or engaging in its ministry, and again, because of its demise, cannot be regarded as a direct ancestor to Reader ministry in today's Church.

# Reader ministry and its origins in the Victorian Church

Reader ministry, in something approaching its contemporary form, began in the second half of the nineteenth century. A brief look at the developments that led to the establishment of this new form of ministry reveal a fascinating story. It might now seem all rather old-fashioned and quaint but in its day it was its own fresh expression of ministry if not of church. Of particular note is just how cautious the Church was in permitting these new ministers to do anything much in the leading of its worship. This is reflected in the fact that Readers did not wear robes until 1941, with the now distinctive 'blue scarf' only becoming standard Reader wear in 1969 adding to, or replacing, a Reader medal.

Let's start, then, by taking as an example one single London parish, St Matthew's, Bethnal Green. During the course of the nine-teenth century there was a massive increase in the population of England with the heavily industrialized North West and London seeing the biggest growth. The online site, *The Clergy of the Church of England Database 1540–1835*,[2] shows in the parish records for St Matthew's, Bethnal Green that James Mayne, the sole clergyman, conducted each year between 1828 and 1831 an average of around:

> 800 christenings, 180 marriages and 670 funerals. The work was unremitting, day after day without a break, with funerals even on Christmas Day. It was also intense. There were days at which he officiated at as many as thirty or even forty christenings, or as many as ten funerals, though only a tiny minority of these involved services in the church as well as in the churchyard
> (<http://journal.ccedb.org.uk/archive/cce_n2.html>)

The population of the parish had trebled in the 30 years from 1800 to 1830 and in the following years 12 more churches would be built within this one original parish of St Matthew. This was quite some expansion and the Church struggled to keep pace with the demands that it faced. The way that parishes were staffed was very different then, of course, and parishes were frequently cared for by curates. Clergy income varied widely and many poorer clergy spent their entire ministry working as perpetual curates on a pitiful stipend, paid by the generally absent vicar out of his parish revenue. James Mayne clearly worked incredibly hard on behalf of the people in his care, but it was a way of ministry that, not surprisingly, proved to be unsustainable.

James Bettley, a freelance architectural historian, interviewed by the Victoria and Albert Museum, says:

> The sheer scale of church building work during this period is really quite hard to imagine now. At the beginning of the 19th century there were about 10,000 parish churches in the country. By 1872, when the survey was carried out, 3204 new churches had been built,

plus 925 existing churches had been entirely rebuilt. That's a total of over 4,000 new churches. There was a survey carried out in 1875, where all the dioceses of England were required to report how many churches had been built or restored at a cost of more than £500 in their diocese, and the total figure for the country came out at 7,892, at a total cost of just over £24 million, which equates to about £1.2 billion in today's money.
(<www.vam.ac.uk/collections/furniture/church_furnish/index.html>)

This illustrates the scale of the need to staff new churches. The church building programme was in part a response to the larger numbers of people living in an area and in part a reflection of the Victorian age's predilection for church building in general – in many instances churches were too large for the needs of their communities and congregations from the day they were opened. Every church that was built had to have the wherewithal to minister to its parishioners, and this massive expansion in both people and buildings was the impetus behind the establishment of Reader ministry. So how did it happen?

In the 1850s the Convocation of Canterbury (the bishops and clergy of the Province of Canterbury meeting as two separate houses) set up a committee charged with the task of considering whether the diaconate might be extended to make it more readily distinguishable from the priesthood, and 'Whether it might be expedient to revive the ancient order of "Readers", as was designed by Archbishop Parker immediately after the Reformation' (*The Chronicles of the Convocation of Canterbury for 1859*, p. 54). With regard to Reader ministry the committee reported to the clergy (the lower house):

> A class of persons is now needed to assist incumbents of populous and scattered parishes in house-to-house visitation, in catechising, and in performing such religious services as may be assigned to them by competent ecclesiastical authority. (p. 55)

Men – for they were, of course, all men – were to be nominated by their incumbent and if they were found suitable they would be commissioned. These first Readers would remain free to resign at any time and the bishop could revoke their commission 'on the grounds of erroneous teaching or immoral conduct' (p. 55). There clearly wasn't an intention in those very early days that this should necessarily be a lifelong role. We'll return to this a little later.

In 1866 the recommendations of this Canterbury report were implemented: lay people could be licensed to a recognized ministerial role in the Church, their licence being to the office of Reader. This fledgling Reader ministry was sanctioned across the whole of the Church of England, in the northern and southern provinces. Its liturgical scope was limited initially to reading lessons at Morning and Evening Prayer (but not at Holy Communion) and saying the litany. Alongside this, of course, Readers were involved in other aspects of ministry from the outset, in teaching and in whatever pastoral work was required of them. From 1884 Readers were permitted to read Morning and Evening Prayer in their entirety (except for the absolution), which meant that for the first time they could lead worship on their own without a clergyman being present, though any preaching that they undertook had to be in unconsecrated buildings. We can see just how cautious this all was; the changes were introduced incrementally, perhaps as people grew used to seeing lay people take on roles that had previously been reserved for those in Holy Orders. We might wonder now why Readers were not permitted to perform a wider range of liturgical functions from the outset. There was not, after all, any theological reason as to why a clergyman was needed to read the offices of Morning and Evening Prayer, or why Readers could not preach in consecrated buildings. This does, however, reflect the spirit of the age, an age that was perhaps more inclined to regulate things that nowadays we wouldn't and also a society that was much more stratified, with everyone knowing his or her place. It is perhaps worth pausing at this point to consider our own attitudes to ministries, roles and functions in church, and the advantages and drawbacks of a 'loosening up' of the regulations about what forms of worship can be led by whom. Let's hold this in mind as we see what happened next.

In the early 1880s there was a further suggestion that a permanent diaconate, and also a sub-diaconate, be established. A report to the Canterbury Convocation in 1882, written in response to this, rejected both of these ideas in favour of a 'two-tier' Reader ministry: 'There should be two distinct classes of Reader with different licences, the lower class to be called "Assistant Readers", the upper class "Readers"' (*The Chronicles of the Convocation of Canterbury for 1884*, p. 3). This was implemented by Frederick Temple as Bishop of London in 1891, when he licensed a number of 'Diocesan' Readers, distinguished by substantially better training from the usual and far more numerous 'Parochial' Readers. The language of 'upper and lower classes' of Readers strikes us nowadays as being rather inappropriate and it illustrates just how much times have changed. We would never now refer to 'different classes' of Readers. While the term might originally have been intended to imply 'categories' rather than 'ranks' it was clear, nonetheless, that there was a significant distinction being made between those who merely 'helped their vicar' in the local parish and those who were considered to be more able and capable of more substantial training and a wider ministry.

It was very much in the spirit of the Victorian reforms, just as it remains a lively part of the questions we face today, to ask what provision might be put in place to enable the clergy to cope – and after much deliberation the answer came in the establishment of Reader ministry. In our own time the question revolves around how clergy and Readers are to be enabled to cope, and answers that could be suggested include 'let Readers do more', perhaps looking after a parish or group of parishes for a stipend or a rent-free house (though this does not provide a complete answer to equally thorny questions about financial resources for ministry). An alternative could be for the Church to extend the exercise of ministerial tasks in some way beyond authorized public ministers to other competent lay people, as is in fact happening 'on the ground' in many places. This would entail an equally thoroughgoing reassessment of the Readers' role if it were not simply to leave Readers feeling displaced or undermined, and with a sense that little or no value is placed on their calling, formation and training.

We can see from history that Reader ministry wasn't so much established as a consequence of the Church acknowledging that lay people have a legitimate and authentic ministerial voice that needed to be given recognition. Rather, it was a response to the question, 'How can we fix a difficult situation?' From our own perspective we might say that the balance of those principles should have been the other way around, but such a value judgement of a former generation is inappropriate and unhelpful. Each age is the product of its own history and context, and expediency and pragmatism are at least as evident in decisions affecting the Church nowadays. But is pragmatism such a great evil? Granted, it can be dismissed as an 'unworthy' concept, and people sometimes consider that to be pragmatic means that one has abandoned principle (and certainly theological principle), but that is not necessarily the case. To be pragmatic is to use one's resources wisely and to seek practical solutions – and this can be about good stewardship. The origin of the word 'pragmatic' is the Greek word *pragma* – it means something that you actually do as distinct from an abstract concept. Pragmatism is a wholesome and worthy part of the development of Reader ministry.

So how were these potential Readers to be identified and prepared? Even in the early days there had been disagreement about the ways in which Readers should be selected and trained. Back in 1859 it had been envisaged that all that would be required in order that someone might become a Reader was an assurance as to their 'Moral character, their religious knowledge, and their efficiency' (*Chronicles for 1859*, p. 55). An interesting exchange took place between the Bishops of Manchester and Carlisle in the Province of York in 1889. The Bishop of Manchester had proposed that Readers should be examined as to their suitability and their knowledge of the Bible and the Book of Common Prayer. The Bishop of Carlisle was having none of it: 'If a clergyman presents to me one of his parishioners and says, "This is a godly man, whom I know well" . . . I am satisfied with that assurance and I admit him to the work' (*York Journal of Convocation 1889*, p. 34).

Well there we are – not a validated academic programme, Director of Reader Training, or Regional Training Partnership in sight! But this exchange shows that the bishops were raising questions about the expertise and spiritual and personal qualities of the candidates. Perhaps the situation in which we find ourselves today – with Readers being rigorously trained, and licensed, while other people conduct worship without undertaking a substantial course of study – provides a close parallel with the different approaches being taken by individual bishops in the early days of Reader ministry. Gradually, although differences remained (and remain) between dioceses, bishops began to establish procedures for selecting and training candidates, and the national Church devised guidelines, recommendations and criteria that all would be expected to follow.

All of this raises an interesting question: at what point does it make sense for the Church to try to define a particular form of ministry: at its beginning; when the practicalities are still being worked out in the light of practice and experience; at some point along the way, when a particular ministry has come to be understood and recognized; or not at all?

We can perhaps see a comparison here with the current understanding by the Church of England that there is a need in today's climate for a different sort of approach to ministry in some places. The response has been to establish 'Pioneer Ministry', an initiative aimed at finding ways of engaging with those outside the Church. Here is something new, intended to meet the needs of the time, intent upon 'declaring the gospel afresh to each generation', yet, by definition, not quite worked out in detail. We need to see, as a Church, how things pan out, setting out the thinking and supporting those who, in responding to God's call, are willing to risk this new way of being a public minister. Planning is a good thing, theological foundations need to be clear, the structures for training and ongoing support need to be there, but there comes a point at which working it all out beforehand as though it were some sort of blueprint to be implemented is likely to be a recipe for disaster. The Church of England will only really be able to assess the impact of this new way of ministering once it is some little way down the track. Indeed it might very well be the case that it defies definition, because once it is possible to describe it in detail the freshness and impetus is lost.

## From the twentieth century to the present day

So now that we have seen how Reader ministry got off the ground, let's note a few milestones along its journey to the present day, not going into great detail but painting with a fairly broad brush a picture of its development.

In 1904 new regulations were drawn up that:

> provided that a Parochial Reader should be licensed, but a Diocesan Reader commissioned . . . Parochial Readers were regarded very much as emergency ministers, inadequately educated, and fitted to minister only in poorer churches, which would not object to ministers of inferior quality, while the Diocesan Readers were regarded as being men of adequate education, or who had been professionally trained for Readership, and so would be acceptable to all congregations.
>
> (King, 1973, p. 113)

It was a distinction that was to remain in place until 1941 when new regulations for Reader ministry decreed that from now on all Readers were to be licensed to hold office not just in their parish, nor even in their diocese, but 'in the Church of God'. This was also the year in which Readers were first allowed to read the epistle during the Eucharist, and to administer Holy Communion (the cup only). These might seem like small additions to the role but, even for these, specific permission had to be given by the bishop to each Reader separately.

Readers were first permitted to preach in consecrated buildings from 1904, though from the chancel step rather than the pulpit (1941) and not at all at services of Holy Communion (1969). The year 1969 also saw the first women admitted to the office of Reader in the Church of England, a ministry into which they entered on equal terms with the men. Ten years later, in 1979, Readers were permitted to bury the dead and to conduct the then rare, and now all but defunct, service known as 'The Churching of Women'. Baptism is not part of the Reader's ministry though they, like any other baptized person, may baptize in an emergency. It remains the case now, as it has always been, that the day-to-day minute detail of what a Reader does is not specifically governed by the Church's formal laws and regulations; rather Canon E4(a) gives general permissions:

> It is lawful for a reader to visit the sick, to read and pray with them, to teach in Sunday school and elsewhere, and generally to undertake such pastoral and educational work and to give such assistance to any minister as the bishop may direct.

In practice, each Reader works out his or her ministry in conjunction with the incumbent in the way that best fits his or her gifts, context and availability, so, as one might expect, the range of activities that Readers are involved in is immensely wide. In addition to church-based tasks it has always been expected that those admitted to the office of Reader would carry a responsibility to witness to their faith in their place of work and in other contexts beyond the parish church. As we will see shortly, this can be an immensely difficult task today for those who work in highly secular or multi-faith organizations.

There has been no change in the liturgical function of the Reader since 1979, though a little bit of tidying up took place in 1988 when they were given permission to administer the consecrated elements of Holy Communion on account of their licence, without any further authorization from the bishop needing to be sought. The whole picture has become much more fluid in recent times as new patterns of ministry have emerged; alongside this now flourishing Reader ministry a whole raft of other permissions and agreements and authorizations has developed in respect of other lay people, and this move has inevitably led to questions about the relationship between the Church's traditional ministries and the various roles that are now being undertaken by a wider range of people. Although this development seems to have come into sharper focus recently it isn't entirely new; the late Rhoda Hiscox traced the start of this development in the life of the Church to around 1970. She wrote:

> Many dioceses now have voluntary pastoral assistants or pastoral workers, men and women who, after training, have been authorized by the bishop to assist the clergy in the pastoral work of the parish. Their duties may include home and hospital visiting, baptismal visits and preparation, and taking Communion to the housebound. Normally their work depends on the needs of the parish, the time they have available, their personal gifts and possibly professional skills, and their initial and continuing training. Some may have a flair for working with young families, others with the dying and bereaved, and others with drug-users or the homeless. Pastoral assistants or workers may take part in church services but they are not licensed to preach. (Hiscox, 1991, p. 107)

She goes on to suggest that this great proliferation of ministries could leave some people feeling as though what they have to offer is somehow second rate because their role is not acknowledged by the giving of a specific badge or title, and asks: 'Are we in danger of stifling and diminishing those who do good by stealth in neighbourly acts of kindness, or by listening to young and old . . . ?' Rhoda Hiscox isn't suggesting that lay people who are not Readers should retreat from the ministerial scene; instead she advocated that Readers take an outward-looking view and resist the temptation to respond in an ungracious or defensive manner when they see other people carrying out 'Reader-type functions'.

In recent years the pace at which new and developing patterns of lay ministry have emerged has increased, with many people now undertaking almost every liturgical function that was previously reserved for the Reader. This has understandably raised issues for Readers about their identity and purpose. Is there still a place for a distinctive Reader ministry in the light of the increasingly fluid picture that is emerging? How permeable does a boundary have to become before it becomes meaningless or disappears altogether? If other lay people are beginning to do much of what was once the preserve of the Reader, might it result in Readers undertaking some tasks within the Church that have traditionally been reserved for those who are ordained? How do Readers themselves feel about all of this? Do they find the current developments threatening or life-giving and energizing? Do Readers feel confident in who they are and in the distinctive nature of what they have to offer?

This isn't the place for a full-scale review of Reader ministry in the Church of England; the Church has undertaken such a review recently and this was published in 2008 as General Synod Report GS1689 *Reader Upbeat: Quickening the Tempo of Reader Ministry in the Church Today*. The findings of that review and the full text of the report can be read on the Church of England's website at <www.cofe.anglican.org/about/gensynod/agendas/gs1689.rtf> or it can be purchased from Church House Bookshop in London.

The picture is inevitably complex. There is a very real sense in which increased lay participation in ministerial tasks, and in particular the burgeoning numbers who are becoming involved in leading worship, including preaching in some cases, is the consequence of both 'bottom-up' and 'top-down' thinking taking place in the Church at the same time. Thinking and trends that emerge in the national Church can take some time to filter down to the local level, and they have to be accepted before they are adopted. Furthermore, no one piece of centralized thinking about ministry is going to find favour in every single parish in the land. Meanwhile, in many places the local church is busy getting on with its own life in pretty much its own way. The shift in thinking that is taking place at grass-roots level right across the Church is a response to the very real needs that are being felt on the ground in parishes of almost every kind. Parishes are being encouraged to identify, nurture and make use of the gifts of their own people and to play their part in finding solutions to the problem of decreasing clergy numbers and the expansion of benefices. This faces the Church with a dilemma that perhaps it doesn't always acknowledge, for in this climate there will always be a tension – which can be a healthy and productive tension – between flexibility, meeting local need and using people's gifts on the one hand, and good church order and governance on the other. It will be important for the Church to articulate and work with this tension, and not simply ignore it, if these two approaches are to be held in balance. Acknowledging the apparent disparity between two different ways of solving the same problem is more likely to mean that the thinking can eventually be joined up in the middle. The alternative is a bit like tunnelling into a mountain from opposite sides and simply hoping that the two ends will eventually meet up in the middle.

At the beginning of every public ministry in the Church of England the person being licensed affirms that they will do all that they can to make known the Christian faith, 'which faith the Church is called upon to proclaim afresh in every generation'. It might be tempting sometimes for people to think: 'Well, I'm here to preach the Christian faith in the ways that I have always done, "preaching it afresh" is for those who are attracted by such initiatives as Fresh Expressions of Church.' But of course this is to miss the point entirely. Reader ministry needs those who have developed the skills of reflective practice, and this means staying alive and alert to all that is happening in the life of the Church and being able to interpret it, work with it and develop it, even though this might sometimes mean stepping beyond our own points of comfort or moving aside in order to make space for approaches that would not naturally be ours.

# 3

# Exploring current practice and Reader ministry

Let's look at some scenarios that draw upon real situations (made suitably anonymous) in the recent life of the Church. Whether the original people involved in these various situations realized it or not – and whether or not they used technical words – the theological points being made mirror very closely the questions about the scope and shape of Reader ministry that have arisen over the past century and a half. Our brief trawl through history has raised the question about what belongs within the ambit of Reader ministry and what can equally well be undertaken by others who have been through a great deal less training. We will also think through some other, related issues to do with Reader ministry. The scenarios are followed by a few questions to start us off as we think through the implications of each.

Ann worships in an isolated parish in a deeply rural multi-parish benefice. Some years ago she volunteered to lead morning worship occasionally in the parish church. James, the vicar, had said how difficult it was for him to provide all the Sunday services that he and the various parishes would like and Ann felt that she had the ability to make a real contribution to the worshipping life of the parish as a lay person. On some Sundays there is Holy Communion, on others worship is shared with the Methodists. Ann usually leads worship once each month. To begin with this was according to the provision for 'A Service of the Word' or Morning Prayer in *Common Worship*, but later, as her confidence grew, she developed a less formal style, using a range of material that she created herself. James worked closely with Ann the first few times that she led worship, and he kept a monitoring eye on things; she clearly had a lot of imagination – more, in fact, than him. He didn't want to be overly controlling, even though it had not initially been his intention or expectation that she should branch out into other forms of worship. Gradually, more people became involved in leading this act of worship and over the past few years it has become a valued part of the parish's life.

This example of a local initiative raises some interesting questions, not least for Reader ministry.

- In your view, was it acceptable for this to happen?
- If so, was it OK only because the vicar couldn't always be there, or was it a good thing anyway?
- There was no Reader in this particular benefice; had there been a Reader should he or she have been asked to lead worship as a matter of course, instead of the vicar accepting Ann's offer?
- The Canons of the Church make provision for people other than clergy and Readers to lead worship when there is no licensed minister available. Should it be that people not only can but should be encouraged to do as Ann did from time to time because it is a good thing of itself rather than a necessity?
- If you think a Reader (had there been one) should have led the worship, would it make a difference to your thinking if the Reader had lived at the other end of this large and scattered benefice, did not really know the people there, and would have had to make a 25-mile round trip to do so?
- Do you think that it would have been acceptable for the vicar to attend this service occasionally when time permitted and sit in the congregation, or should he have led the worship himself if available? Or, as he was there to preside at Holy Communion on other Sundays, should he have stayed away and left them to it?
- Are there any other issues that this raises for you?

Asking a number of Readers about this scenario revealed the extent to which we often want to say 'Yes' to two seemingly opposing points of view. Some had no problem with anyone at all leading and devising worship, others felt that if people with minimal training were to lead worship it should be either a recognized form provided by the Church of England, or something put together with (or overseen by) people who are trained and experienced in ministry. Others were clear that all ministry must be undertaken by those who have been selected, trained and authorized by the wider Church. Liz said:

We have a few people in our benefice who would like to lead non-Eucharistic services. The vicar is very certain that they won't be permitted to do this. People are allowed to take parts of a service but not plan and lead the whole thing unless they do what she calls 'a significant amount of training'. Ministry is the task of those who have been given a public role. The two or three people who want to be more involved in leading worship would say, 'I have a lot to offer and I don't need to be trained to do it.' The response of the incumbent is that if you're not prepared to align yourself with the Church's structures you don't have the authority to minister. I find myself agreeing with her.

Dave is an RE teacher, a gifted speaker with a good knowledge and understanding of scripture. At a PCC meeting someone suggested to Jane, the vicar, that Dave might be invited to preach from time to time on a Sunday morning. The PCC was divided. Someone said that while they had no difficulty with the idea that Dave might have something useful to contribute, he shouldn't be allowed to preach because 'it could open the floodgates and we'd have all sorts of people wanting to stand up in church and say something'. No, if Dave were to preach regularly, some of them said, he'd need to train as a Reader. Jane had mentioned the possibility of Reader ministry to Dave some months earlier but he had said that he didn't feel called to it, though he did feel called to preach. Someone else suggested that perhaps Dave might be asked to give a talk rather than preach a sermon, but Jane said that if he were to do this regularly he would in fact be preaching, and it would be rather dishonest simply to call it something different. Norman and Ben are Readers: Norman thought that no one should be permitted to preach regularly unless they had a recognized, public ministry, and he quoted Canon Law in support of his argument. Ben, on the other hand, felt that the Canons of the Church sometimes needed to catch up with developments at grass-roots level rather than hold them back. Some members of the PCC couldn't see what all the fuss was about.

- Where do your sympathies lie here? If your immediate response is to say that they lie with all concerned, how might this particular circle be squared?

- What do you think would be a good and appropriate outcome?
- Would you be more in support of Norman or of Ben? Can you say why?
- How might the Church respond when someone appears to be gifted in one particular aspect of Reader ministry but doesn't feel called to the whole?

Again there was a difference of view among Readers. Liz flagged up just how difficult it can be to establish, and expect people to adhere to, a clear set of regulations that govern just who has permission to do what. We saw that she was adamant that those who are to take a significant role in leading worship ought to train as Readers. In response to the question, 'How might the Church respond when someone feels called to one aspect of ministry, but not to the whole of it?', she replied:

> You can't just allow anyone to preach; there's a certain obligation to ensure that whatever is said is acceptable. But if a parish is sure that someone would be excellent as a preacher perhaps there ought to be a way found of permitting this aspect of ministry to flourish and the Church shouldn't lose those people because they don't feel called to the whole of Reader ministry. I find this really difficult because there's a lot of contradictory stuff around with regard to lay ministry and where it should go. You can see both sides to so much of it.

This highlights an important complexity within the life of the Church at the present time. The Church of England is bound by a carefully crafted set of rules and regulations that all are expected to follow. Some of these are expressed in the form of the Canons of the Church and their purpose is to ensure the good ordering and governance of the Church. They were framed in order that the Church might be as sure as it can be that the quality of what is being delivered is high and consistent, and were definitely not set in place to limit the effective spread of the gospel, or to hinder the mission of the Church. Our dilemma here is that some of the most vibrant and effective forms of outreach and evangelism, and some of the most significant growth, appears to be happening in places where local gifts are being closely matched with local need, and where new and different ways of engaging with the gospel message, far from simply being tolerated, are being encouraged. A number of Readers were sympathetic to the pro-Dave position and found that it reflected the practice of their own parish.

Chris's response was, 'If that were to happen in our church – someone suitably gifted came along and the vicar and PCC were happy with it – I think it would be fine.'

Les's own story chimes with this rather freer approach:

I sit very loosely to things like this. I come from a Free Church background where many more people are involved. I don't think we should necessarily insist on all the training in advance. I was converted at 18 and thrown into preaching at the age of 19. Someone mentioned that the local Methodist circuit was short of local preachers. I said I'd be interested – a short time later the Methodist plan dropped through the letter box with my name on it in three places. I started training as a Methodist Local Preacher but moved to London where I attended, and did some preaching at, the London City Mission, which had about 100 mission halls. If the person in charge was happy with your preaching they invited you back. I learnt through doing it; we can sometimes make it all so difficult that people never get started. If I'd not started off in little country chapels I might not have taken the Reader route later on. Back in York I attended a C of E church and took an eight-week preaching course led by my vicar. Gradually I began to feel that as an Anglican I ought to get myself properly qualified and this led to Reader training.

If we give people the opportunity to do things without having to pre-qualify they might realize that they've got gifts and go from there. This doesn't mean that everyone would be appropriate and there has to be discernment within the church – and appropriate oversight. This happens in my current church where we have a group called 'Word from the pew'. A small group of people meet with the vicar and me and they are then invited to preach at an evening service. Sometimes they set about it with great trepidation! If we were to be faced with an interregnum we would have as a resource a competent group of people who can help lead worship and it won't all fall on people like me – there's a limit to what you can do. Anything that helps people to get started is a good thing. The vicar spoke to the bishop about it, so it's had his authority – it isn't a subversive thing. We don't ask for volunteers, though; the vicar approaches people. Before we began this the vicar asked me how I would feel about it – he wanted to know whether I'd be upset that they were being asked to do this, but I thought it was an excellent idea and have given it my full support.

Jenny, too, thinks that opportunities to preach can be extended to suitably equipped lay people, as long as this is not on a very regular basis:

During the summer holidays all the people who make up the team that runs the holiday club lead morning worship on a Sunday. They are able people who are used to doing this sort of thing on children's camps. I asked the vicar if we could get them together to have them in reserve as preachers. We meet once per term to discuss how they might go about it and some of them preach at our afternoon service. It works very well. My understanding is that we can use them on a very occasional basis but that if we use them more than that then they ought to be Readers. We do have to make sure, though, that people don't go off at a tangent. The same is true of Fresh Expression services; the Church goes through new forms of liturgy line by line at General Synod but then we sometimes see people writing all sorts of things into worship that they have devised themselves.

Another (anonymous!) Reader made the same point: 'I heard some very dodgy doctrine in a Eucharist once and asked the curate leading it where it had come from. He said that he had made it up.'

Clare has been a Reader in her parish for ten years. She has always robed for the main Sunday worship. Jack, the vicar who has supported her in her ministry for many years retired some months ago and has recently been replaced by Will. Clare has been enthusiastic about some of his proposed changes, but she is struggling with others, especially his suggestion that ministers only robe when they are leading a significant part of the service. Will has tried to help Clare understand his position on all of this; he feels

strongly that the differentiation between minister and congregation needs to be lessened. In many ways Clare has a lot of time
for Will; he is kind and keen and she is happy that he wants to
try to move the parish forward. Although she had grown very
fond of Jack over the years she could see that he had run out of
steam long before when it came to mission. Nonetheless, she feels
as though her role as a public minister of the Church is being
'watered down'. Clare had thought that she would always have
a role as a Reader at evensong; she had led BCP evensong for a
small congregations for several years. Will, though, had recently
suggested that they abandon the evening service altogether
between October and March as it was costly to heat the church
for such a tiny congregation. He suggested that they meet in the
parish meeting room instead. Clare thought that this really
wasn't adequate and she was beginning to feel quite distressed;
she was starting to think that she should perhaps speak with the
bishop about the possibility of moving to a different parish.

- What issues does this story raise for you about the relationship
  between a Reader and her or his incumbent?
- How significant for you is the recognition and affirmation of
  Clare's ministry within the parish community? Do you identify
  more with Will or Clare with regard to the appropriateness of the
  ministry team always sitting apart from the congregation?
- Some people appreciate the use of robes while others find them
  to be outmoded and either irrelevant or actually unhelpful. The
  Church of England still requires ministers to robe for some worship. What reasons can you identify for or against the wearing of
  robes in different forms of worship?
- Both Will and Clare are passionate about the well-being of the
  parish. Clare understands that change must come but she finds
  Will's pace and some of his ideas difficult. How might Will and
  Clare work through some of the tensions towards a positive outcome, both for their relationship and for the parish as a whole?
  Might there be some things that each can learn from the other?
- Clare has developed a particular ministry towards the small evensong congregation and she values leading worship for them on
  a regular basis; in fact it is known in the parish that this is 'her
  service'. Another Reader said at a recent meeting that he regrets

the demise of evensong because it deprives him of an important opportunity to lead a service without feeling like the 'vicar's helper'. How do you see changing patterns of worship affecting Reader ministry? On balance do you find that the changes open or close possibilities for creative Reader ministry?

This scenario raises issues that touch on the nature of Reader ministry and its permanence.

> Two people, Gordon and June, are talking about their ministry with a mutual friend, Alec. June has an active ministry as a Reader. Gordon was also admitted as a Reader some years ago, but he became disaffected with the Church and his ministry petered out. Alec says, 'Just tell me something – once you are made a Reader, is that for ever, or can you stop?' June says, 'Yes – it stays with you until your dying day, even if you move churches or finish doing anything active for the Church. I'm just as much a Reader when I'm asleep or on holiday as when I'm consciously doing things as a minister.' Gordon says, 'I really don't see it like that. I used to be a Samaritan, and when I gave it up, that was it. It's the same with my Reader ministry. I'm not a Reader any more.'

- People are only admitted to the order of Reader once, though they may be licensed on a number of occasions. In what ways do you consider that it makes sense to speak of this one-off admission as conferring a lifelong ministry and identity upon a Reader?
- Is it possible to stop being a Reader? If so, what could bring it to an end?

Here is a different type of scenario:

> Darren has Asperger's syndrome; he is a graduate who is on the high-functioning end of the autistic spectrum. Darren is very involved in the life of his parish and feels called to some form of public ministry. He knows that there are some things he would not be able to do, especially on the organizational front and says that he definitely couldn't cope with being a stipendiary priest. Darren is aware that he doesn't always pick up on clues and signals in conversations and in social settings. He says that people often think he is slightly 'odd' – a highly subjective word that we

might prefer to avoid in the Church, but one that people still use casually. In today's culture we tend to name and give labels to things that depart from a so-called 'norm'. This can sometimes be helpful (e.g. a diagnosis of dyslexia can liberate someone who struggles with printed text), but there are times when such an approach can lead to lowered expectations, exclusion and stigma. Darren fears that people, especially strangers, might find his condition a distraction and that it might inhibit them from readily accepting his ministry. He feels that Reader ministry would perhaps be a better fit for what he can realistically offer than ordained ministry. Meanwhile Darren, together with his parish and diocese, is struggling to discern an appropriate way of enabling him, as a committed, prayerful, intelligent and enthusiastic candidate of 24, to answer his sense of call and to fulfil his potential as a minister.

- Does this description of norms and labels fit in with your own experience of attitudes in society and Church?
- The Church is (appropriately) governed by the same anti-disability legislation as the rest of society and must not, therefore, discriminate against people on account of their medical conditions. People with this syndrome have (in varying degrees) difficulty in understanding the thoughts and feeling of others, and this can affect the ways in which they relate and communicate. What challenges might Darren's condition pose for those who need to interpret the Church's selection criteria in the light of his candidature?
- The media caricature of the vicar or minister has sometimes (and one might say unhelpfully) been of a rather eccentric misfit. Do you think nevertheless that 'unusual' people might bring real gifts to the Church? How might such gifts enhance the Church's life and ministry?
- Whatever conclusion you come to about Darren's candidature, can you think of other things that might – perhaps unfairly or inappropriately – be a block to the acceptance of someone's ministry?

The point is that we cannot look at the story of Reader ministry over the past 150 years or so and see it as culminating in some sort of perfect state today. Yes, to a great extent, its terms have been defined by central church authority – including decisions of the bishops and

Convocations, and the text of Measures and Canons that have been through the national synodical process. But Reader ministry is also formed and shaped by local experience; by creative, experimental, imaginative initiatives; by the response to locally identified needs, and through discovering and exercising God-given gifts. Reader ministry has always been, and continues to be, on a journey. Anyone who engages in Reader ministry, or who (whether lay or ordained) has any contact with it, potentially has a part in discerning and developing the Reader ministry of the future – which is an exciting prospect, full of possibilities.

# Part 2

# EXPLORING YOUR CALLING, SELECTION AND TRAINING

# 4

# Discerning a call to Reader ministry

## Vocation in the Bible

One of the essential characteristics of God is that he calls. Throughout the Bible, time and time again we find God calling out to people, drawing them onwards into the life that he yearns for them to have.

The word 'call' in Hebrew is *qara'* and is a very general word used to describe many different forms of communication for which we need a range of English words. It can be used for naming ('God called the light Day, and the darkness he called Night', Gen. 1.5), to refer to someone being summoned personally ('Then Moses said to the Israelites: See, the Lord has called by name Bezalel son of Uri son of Hur, of the tribe of Judah; he has filled him with divine spirit, with skill, intelligence, and knowledge in every kind of craft', Exod. 35.30–31), and even for crying out ('Out of the depths I cry to you, O Lord!', Ps. 130.1). This last example is particularly interesting, as it illustrates the way in which the same word in Hebrew is used for our crying out to God as for God's calling to us.

In essence, then, 'calling' is about communication. Just as we cry out to God in the hope that he will hear and respond, so God calls out to us in the hope that we will hear and respond. We can be sure, therefore, that God is calling out to each one of us, and just as we hope that our cries to God will result in his doing something for us, so also does God's call to us have within it an expectation of action. This pattern of calling and responding continues into the New Testament. One of the first things that Jesus did in his ministry was to call people to follow him, something which he continued to do throughout his life.

Calling, however, can take many different guises. Sometimes in the Bible people were called to a complete change of life. Abraham, for example, was called to leave everything behind and to journey onwards to a destination as yet undisclosed ('Go from your country and your kindred and your father's house to the land that I will show you', Gen. 12.1). In the same way, Jesus' first disciples were called to leave everything behind and to 'follow' with little indication of what this would entail ('And he said to them, "Follow me, and I will make you fish for people"', Mark 1.17). Both of these callings were to a completely different life.

Other people were called to a task, which, though life-changing at the time, was limited and came to an end. Take, for example, Jonah, a prophet who was called to proclaim doom to Nineveh (a call which he strenuously avoided as long as he could). Once his task was fulfilled, however – and the people of Nineveh had, much to Jonah's surprise, heard his message and repented – we can presume that Jonah went back to his normal life and continued doing what he was doing before. Again, the call to Isaiah the prophet, in Isaiah 6.1–11, seems to be to a short-term, not long-term, calling. Isaiah 6 records Isaiah's remarkable vision of God in the Temple, with the end of God's cloak (his train) filling the Temple and the seraphs flying around and crying out that God is holy. Within this, God asks who he can send and Isaiah volunteers: 'Here I am, send me.' The task God gives him is confusing but also very specific – he is to tell the people to keep listening but not to comprehend, to look but not understand. He appears to have an immediate task to prevent the people from understanding (why this is, still remains unclear), but which, once achieved, would probably have been over.

Both of these examples of short-term tasks involve prophets who were called to specific action as a part of their general calling of being a prophet. This is important, because it reminds us that 'vocation' occurs at many different levels. God calls us in ways that transform our whole lives and demand that we will never be the same again, but God also calls us to tasks (both great and small), which might disrupt what we are doing already, but ultimately fit into it.

What this means is that God is calling us at every point of our lives. Sometimes that call will be to a large life-transforming change of direction, but at other times (and more often) it will be to specific tasks that lie alongside other vocations we already have. In short, we do not have *a* God-given vocation but God-given *vocations*, and we must be constantly on the alert for the new ways in which God may be calling us.

You can be confident, therefore, that God *is* calling you and draw-ing you further on into your life of faith. What is less clear is what God is calling you to. It might be to an enormous life-changing vocation or it may be to a new vocation which lies alongside a number of other vocations to which you have already been called.

The word 'vocation' is used of more things than public ministry: people talk of a vocation to teach, for example, or to be a doctor. It is also used for a whole range of 'hands-on' skills and occupa-tions for which 'vocational training' is given. Many of these reflect jobs within society that have an element of providing a service for others. This is a recognition of the fact that a sense of calling is something that exists in the whole of life and not just in church. Thus we all have multiple vocations which include being (for ex-ample to be in relationship as mother, father, sister, brother, daughter, son, friend, partner, etc.) as well as doing (for example to be a doctor, teacher, carer, minister . . .).

Of course, when we use the word vocation within the Church we often use it to refer to ministry, and not only that but to refer to a particular role within ministry (e.g. Reader, pastor, ordained minister). One of the challenges that people often encounter is how they know *what* it is that they are being called to by God.

## Discerning God's call

Even within the Church of England people have different views about how to recognize when people are 'called' by God to public ministry within the Church.

- Some say that there must be a very real, personal sense of being called by God to undertake this particular task for, with and on behalf of the Church;
- others are more interested in whether someone has the skill or ability to 'do the job' required of a public minister, in this case a Reader.

There are of course a range of perspectives in between these two; but the range itself is valuable. We need Readers who have both the depth of conviction that God is calling them to Reader ministry and the skills to carry out this calling effectively.

When we talk about vocation, we often use the language of discernment. Discernment involves taking a serious look at all the possibilities and all the options that are open to you, and thinking them through with a few simple questions in mind:

- What do I feel God drawing me towards in my life?
- Of all the ways of serving God that I can identify in my situation and context, which of them seems to be the most life-giving both for myself and those around me?
- What particular gifts have I been given and how can these best be used in the service of others, of Christ and of the Church?
- What needs do I perceive both in the Church and outside it, and in what way can I respond to these needs?
- What do I enjoy doing and what gives me the most energy?
- What do other people most often ask me to do; does this tell me something about where they think my gifts lie?

These are the sorts of questions that all Christian people ask to help them discern how best to live their Christian life. So, in a very real sense, discerning a call to Reader ministry is simply an extension of the ordinary ongoing reassessing and reappraising of one's walk with God that is part of the life of every Christian disciple.

The first part of discerning a call involves a process in which we should all be involved as a part of our everyday walk with God. This involves asking questions about what God wants of us and how we might best use our skills as a part of our everyday discipleship.

## Being honest with ourselves

It is also important within the discernment process to be honest with ourselves about why we are seeking a particular form of ministry. People's motives, even if honourable, are always likely to be mixed and may sometimes be unrealistic; it is vital to face up to every aspect of our sense of vocation. Unfortunately, as with many things in life, vocation is affected by some of the less attractive aspects of our human nature, some of which we acknowledge, others of which are hidden under the surface and not even identified by us as being present. These might include:

- self-serving – a desire for recognition or status;
- a 'need to be needed';
- a need to control;
- competition with others;
- unwillingness to be led.

It is understandable that those seeking ministry are likely to want to present their 'best face', but it is essential that anyone who is seeking to minister publicly within and on behalf of the Church looks at all their motives and acknowledges before God those aspects of themselves that are perhaps less honourable. It is probably true to say that no one is 100 per cent pure/altruistic/God-centred in their motives. All have fallen short of the glory of God, yet God uses all sorts of people to further the work of the Kingdom. The 'perfect candidate' is almost certainly someone who is not perfect but who is aware of their imperfections and has learnt to face them.

## How do I know whether Reader ministry might be right for me?

The next step in the discernment process is to begin to identify whether Reader ministry is in fact the ministry to which God is calling you. Without doubt one of the hardest aspects of working through any vocation to ministry is the question of how I know whether this particular ministry is right for me.

Reader ministry finds its expression in many different forms within our churches. Indeed, one of the challenges of talking about Reader ministry is that it can differ from person to person, local context to local context and diocese to diocese. Nevertheless, a basic definition of Reader ministry is often considered to involve a preaching and teaching ministry exercised within a pastoral context. Potential Readers, therefore, need to ensure that they feel comfortable with both aspects of the Readers' role:

- preaching and teaching
- pastoral context.

It is important to remember that you don't have to be good at either preaching and teaching or at pastoral work yet – don't forget that Reader training is there to help you to grow into the role of Reader –

but you do need to be able to face both aspects of Reader ministry without too much horror!

As well as checking that you are comfortable with the major features of Reader ministry it is also valuable to ensure that your sense of vocation is not to another form of ministry, such as ordination.

## How do I begin to decide?

Many Readers with substantial and effective ministries can recall facing questions about what kind of ministry they are being called to and whether they are the right person for that ministry in the early days. There is always a balance to be found between rushing in too quickly, and letting ideas chase around one's head for too long. Either approach can be counterproductive. Sooner or later, though, the issue must be aired if it is to be resolved. There are a number of things that people can do to help themselves work through their questions. Probably the most important thing to do is to pray about them over a period of time, both before and while doing some or all of the following:

- Read through the Church's selection criteria (see pp. 50–1 below) and think through or write down the extent to which you think you fulfil them. Be as honest as you can be.
- Write about your hopes and fears, especially the ones that seem the most exciting or the most frightening and strange. The process of writing things down can of itself sometimes be a way of seeing things in a clearer light, as can drawing ideas and images when it is hard to find the right words. Some people are helped by writing a 'conversation' between God and themselves as a way of discerning what they ought to do.
- Share them with a few close family and friends, and ask for an honest response.
- Seek out a Reader to talk to, not necessarily someone who has been licensed for a long time who might have forgotten just how powerful such thoughts can be, but perhaps someone fairly new to ministry, or maybe someone still in training. Sharing thoughts with another, perhaps someone who does not know you very well, can help to bring a fresh sense of perspective, and discovering

that others have been down the same path before you is generally hugely reassuring.

- Talk to someone whom you consider to be wise, and who knows you well, about your hopes and fears and thoughts. (Examples of this kind of person include your spiritual director or soul friend, a prayer partner, someone in leadership within your church.)
- Discuss it all with your incumbent (i.e. the vicar or rector of your parish).

Here are some of the most common areas that might need to be addressed by those wondering whether to apply to train for Reader ministry.

## Capability

Would Reader ministry demand things of me that I could not do? This is a hard question for any of us to answer because few of us can do now the same things as we can do after months and years of training. It might be more productive to ask whether you are the kind of person who enjoys being stretched, learning new things and trying out new skills. Readers are a group of people to whom the Church has entrusted parts of its public ministry. You do not have to be ready now to undertake this role, but you do need to be someone who is willing to learn new ideas and approaches and who is ready to undertake whatever it is that the Church needs doing in each generation. All of us will from time to time feel as though more is being asked of us than we can possibly have the skills, knowledge, training and inner resources to deliver. This is OK! The danger comes not when we feel out of our depth, but when we become so self-sufficient that we stop learning new ways of doing things and engaging with new ideas. We do not need to be endlessly capable, but we do need to be endlessly interested and willing to be drawn into new ways of being and thinking.

## Time

Do I realistically have enough time to give to Reader ministry and training? Both training for Reader ministry and the exercise of it will make significant demands upon your time. Most Reader candidates are already significantly involved in the life of their church and it is likely that some responsibilities will have to be laid down in order to make time for the requirements of training. The capacity of people to absorb additional demands varies greatly from one person to another, but it is important to say here that it is the long experience of the Church that God does not call people to a ministry that is not sustainable or that puts existing commitments, to marriage, family, professional life or health, under intolerable pressure.

## Worthiness and finding an appropriate sense of self

Am I good enough to do this?

All Christian people are called to live lives that follow the example of Jesus – and all fall short. Being a follower of Jesus is not about belonging to a club whose members think that they are good; to be a Christian is to be a witness to the good news of Jesus in the midst of our failure. There is an important distinction to be made here between having on the one hand an appropriate sense of being an unworthy servant of the Lord, and on the other hand a lack of personal self-worth that has less to do with humility and more to do with an inability to recognize that we each have an intrinsic value as a much loved child of God. People sometimes get these badly muddled; it is essential that those offering themselves for the Church's ministry think this distinction through in order that they might be free to minister to others effectively. If this is left unaddressed it can easily lead people to use ministry as a covert (though often unrealized) means of seeking ministry *from* others under the guise of offering ministry *to* others. We are all unworthy, that is the reality, but if we are hampered by an inappropriately self-condemnatory image we will struggle to grasp the liberating power of the gospel, both for ourselves and for others.

On the other hand, sometimes, in the early days of thinking about whether or not they should offer for Reader ministry, people become quite focused upon themselves. '*I'm* going to be a Reader!' Perhaps the call of the prophet Isaiah has something to say to us here. You might have noticed that when people read aloud the account of the calling of Isaiah from chapter 6, the emphasis is sometimes: 'Then I heard the voice of the Lord saying, "Whom shall I send, and who will go for us?" And I said, *"Here* am I; *send* me!"'' But on other occasions it is read as: 'Here am *I*; send *me*!' The same thing can be seen when people sing the hymn, 'I, the Lord of Sea and Sky'. The question posed by the chorus, 'Here I am, Lord, *is it I*, Lord?' seems to have entered many people's consciousness as, 'Here I am, Lord, *it is I*, Lord'. The questioning and self-offering has been replaced by an assertion that sets the individual at the centre of the picture.

Being part of the public ministry of the Church is not just about self-proclamation, it is about responding to the invitation of God in Christ to share in that ongoing work of a creation that will groan with longing until the end of time (Rom. 8.22). But at the same time our individuality is important; it matters to the Church and its ministry because it matters to God. It is the people we are, with all our history, our experience, our gifts, our faults and our failings who are being called into God's service; real, living, praising, worshipping, sinning, repenting people, each with a story of redemption to proclaim as part of the Church's, the world's – and ultimately of course, God's – bigger story of redemption.

## Family support

Does my family support me?

Of course, your family does not need to have the same degree of enthusiasm for the idea of your entering Reader ministry as you do, but if they are entirely resistant to the idea then your time as a Reader will be fraught with difficulty and possibly also conflict. While there are some who would argue that people ought not to be recommended for training for an authorized ministry in the Church if they have a spouse or partner who does not share their faith, the reality is that there are very many families in this situation who accommodate one another's beliefs and hopes in a manner that is fully supportive while not being totally shared. What is important at this point, however, is that you ensure that your calling to Reader ministry is not going to put an unbearable strain upon your closest relationships; beyond this you will need to do what many people in ministry do which is to work it out as you go along, balancing your calling and enthusiasms with the needs and concerns of those you love.

## Seeking the support of the local church

Do my incumbent, PCC and local congregation support me?

It is vitally important that all those who are seeking to be selected for training for the Church's public ministry have the support of the local church. A central tenet of the Church of England's approach to ministry is that all ministry is done within a local context; it is not possible to be an itinerant minister in the Church. One of the key aspects of the Church of England's self-understanding is that it is an episcopal Church; it is led by bishops, with the diocesan bishop being responsible for all the ministry that takes place within the diocese. This means that all those who engage in public ministry are responsible to the bishop, and that while at its heart all ministry is carried out in Christ's name, in organizational terms it is the bishop who has oversight. In other words, all those in permanent, public ministry within the Church of England should have the bishop's permission to minister. Of course most Readers will not have day-to-day contact with their bishop but will relate to the incumbent of the parish or benefice in which they are to serve. This does not undermine the model of episcopal leadership, but is the way in which it is worked out in the life of the Church. It will be expected in almost every case that the candidate has the full and enthusiastic support of the incumbent, who will be asked to write a reference as part of the process of selection. In addition it would be usual for the candidate to have the strong support of the PCC, and it is the norm for a motion to be passed at a meeting at which the candidate is not present, stating that this is the case.

So why say that the incumbent must be supportive in *almost* every case? This raises an interesting question about the nature of Reader ministry. Reader ministry is, almost by definition, collaborative, because, with a few exceptions, Readers minister alongside their incumbent – and often alongside other members of a ministry team, which will include people who are both lay and ordained. In order for this relationship to work, it is important that wherever possible the incumbent, the PCC, and ideally the congregation as a whole, are supportive of the Reader's vocation and ministry within the church.

This raises the question of whether, if someone feels called to offer themselves for selection for training as a Reader and they happen to worship in a parish where the incumbent is not personally supportive of Reader ministry, the individual must lay aside their sense of calling and continue to take an active part in their parish in the ways that are permitted. Or should they seek an alternative place in which to minister? The answer to this will not be the same

in every case. It may be that the candidate will train on the understanding that he or she will be licensed to a church other than that
in which they began the process of discernment – and some dioceses
have a general policy of telling potential candidates from the outset that they may be deployed in a new parish or setting when they
are eventually licensed. Or it might be the case that someone would
need to move to a different parish and spend some time there, getting to know the people, before seeking to apply to train as a Reader.
Such instances are rare but not unknown, and they can lead to real
heart-searching on the part of all involved if a resolution is to be
found that neither leaves the individual feeling as though their call
has been dismissed or negated, nor leads to a sense of uprooted-
ness and loss. The worst possible outcome is for the incumbent and
PCC to express their support and for the candidate to complete
training satisfactorily and be licensed, only to find that their ministry is never thereafter incorporated into the life of the parish.
What this highlights is the importance of ensuring that you have
an honest conversation with your incumbent both before you put
yourself forward for selection and at regular intervals during your
training so that you can both be confident that you have shared
expectations of your future ministry.

## Working with the selection criteria

At some point in the process of discerning your call, you will reach
a point where you begin to identify Reader ministry as an area to
which you may be being called. You have worked through the issues
with various people, and feel that having a part in the preaching/
teaching and pastoral heart of Reader ministry is something that
either attracts you or at least doesn't horrify you. At this point, then,
it is valuable to look at the national criteria laid down for Readers.

The Church of England produces criteria for selection for all its
authorized public ministries. There is considerable similarity between
the general descriptors of the criteria for ordained and Reader ministry, but the detail, outworking and interpretation of these will
vary according to the ministry being considered. Criteria for Reader
Ministry as set out by the Church of England (Selection for Reader
Ministry, ABM Policy Paper No. 7, 1998) are shown in the box on
pp. 50–1.

### Ministry in the Church of England

Candidates must be baptized and confirmed and regular communicants of the Church of England who are familiar with its traditions and practices. They must complete the necessary disclosure statement in connection with the House of Bishops' Policy on Child Protection before undergoing the diocesan selection procedure.

### Vocation

Candidates should be able to speak of their own sense of vocation to ministry and mission, referring both to personal conviction and to the extent to which others have confirmed it. Their sense of vocation should be obedient, realistic and informed.

### Faith

Candidates should show an understanding of the Christian faith and a desire to deepen that understanding. They should demonstrate personal commitment to Christ and a capacity to communicate the gospel.

### Spirituality and worship

Candidates should show evidence of commitment to a spiritual discipline which involves individual and corporate prayer and worship. Their spiritual practice should be such as to sustain and energize them in their daily lives.

### Personality and character

Candidates should be sufficiently mature and stable to show that they can sustain the demanding role of a minister and to face change and pressure in a flexible and balanced way. They should be seen to be people of integrity.

### Relationships

Candidates should demonstrate self-awareness and self-acceptance as a basis for developing open and healthy personal and pastoral relationships as ministers.

**Potential for training**

Candidates should be capable of undertaking satisfactorily a course of study and ministerial preparation with an open and enquiring mind.

**Leadership and collaboration**

Candidates should show the potential to offer wise leadership in the Church community and to some extent beyond it. They should also show ability and willingness to co-operate with other ministers and to work as team members as well as leaders.

These criteria exist for a number of reasons:

- they enable candidates and those working with them to prepare for selection;
- they inform advisers, who undertake their work on behalf of both their diocesan bishop and the wider Church, about what qualities to look out for in a potential Reader candidate;
- they play a vital role in ensuring consistency across the Church in the recommendation of candidates;
- they provide an outline of the theological framework upon which Reader ministry, as one aspect of the Church's public ministry, is based.

In short, the criteria provide guidelines which allow all those involved in selection, whether as advisers or as candidates, to be confident that the decisions made are fair and equitable.

## The selection procedure

So far in this chapter we have explored the idea of how you can begin to discern whether your sense of inner prompting is leading you to Reader ministry or not. It is important to recognize, however, that the vocational process is two-sided. God calls, and once we have heard and discerned this call we offer ourselves for ministry. The challenging fact, however, is that our vocation also has to be received. For example, there is no point insisting that God has called me to visit people in the parish if no one in the parish wants me to visit them. The purpose of Reader selection is to test whether others within the Church (who know the diocese and Reader ministry well) can also perceive within you a vocation to Reader ministry. Our own personal acceptance of our vocation is only a part of the picture; it also needs to be accepted by others.

## What happens if the answer is no?

One of the hardest features of a discernment process occurs when someone's vocation is not accepted by the church or community to which it is offered. If this should happen to you it is very important, once you are able to, to view this decision in its proper light. First, remember that such a decision is not saying that God is not calling you at all – we established above that God calls everyone all of the time – it simply means that your calling is not to Reader ministry but to something else.

You need, therefore, to find a way of discerning what it is that God is calling you to. It can often be very hard to move onwards to this discernment process again. You will just have spent a long time discerning in order to get as far as the selection process for Reader ministry and the thought of (what will feel like) going back again will be hard. You may also feel bruised and hurt by the experience, which may feel like rejection (even though it is not).

In this situation, a few guidelines may be helpful:

- Give yourself time. You do not have to know *now* what God wants from you. Sometimes the period of waiting is vital to help us grow into the person that God wants us to be.
- Be gentle with yourself. You are allowed to feel hurt, but don't allow this hurt to diminish your self-esteem. God loves you for who you are.
- Be honest with yourself. You don't need to tell anyone else unless it helps, but sometimes it can be helpful to be brutally honest with yourself about your inner motives. Ask yourself whether there might be anything to be learned from this experience (of course the answer may be no).
- Most importantly of all, seek out someone who can help you to reflect on this whole experience. It may be your incumbent, spiritual director, soul friend or someone else entirely. In fact, sometimes it can help to talk to someone entirely outside of the process and to see what emerges from your conversation about your experience.

## What happens if the answer is yes?

Sometimes the answer yes can be as daunting (if not more so) than the answer no. Some people offer themselves for ministry in the hope that God or the Church will say no and then discover that they have to live with the yes! As after a 'no' answer, give yourself time, be gentle with yourself, be honest with yourself and find someone to talk to (in this case an already licensed Reader or one who is training might be helpful). Once you begin training you will enter a whirl of new ideas and new ways of looking at things. It helps to be as ready as you can be!

## Some stories of people who felt called to Reader ministry

Now read what prompted some very different Readers to seek this ministry. It doesn't happen now quite as it did for Bobby in the early 1980s!

### Bobby – a Reader for 23 years

The local vicar was the Scout master; he took us to church and if you could read a psalm and sing a scale you joined the choir. My family didn't go to church but I sang in the choir and eventually became a server. I wanted to be a vicar when I was at school but my father was a miner and couldn't afford to keep me, so I left school and became a nurse as it was a caring profession. Much later when the children were young we didn't go to church for a while because they made a noise, but eventually I returned. One day someone asked whether I would stand for election as a churchwarden. I gradually became more involved in the life of the church, reading and so on. One day, out of the blue, the vicar said that he had asked the bishop about me being a Reader; this was followed by a letter from the bishop: 'Congratulations, I am delighted to hear that you are going to be a Reader.' That was it. There was no interview or selection procedure. I worked with a local tutor for two years and I put all my heart and soul into it. Being a nurse linked the whole thing for me; everyone at the hospital knew that I was a licensed Reader – I was a bridge between people there and church. People ask when I decided to become a Reader, but I didn't, I just grew into it. I was a very slow-growing plant!

## Dianne – a Reader for three years

I had nearly died during the birth of my first child and during that experience I felt as though I was in the company of someone who knew me totally. When I recovered I knew that something was missing from my life. I went to church and my faith and that of my husband (who initially only came to church to please me) began to grow, though in very different ways. Eventually I wanted to read and learn more and grow so I talked with a friend who said, 'You need to take time out to listen to what God is asking of you.' But I didn't like what I felt God was asking of me, which was to stand up and do something more. I wondered about Reader ministry, whether this was a good match and someone made a remark about my becoming a Reader. I found out later that they were being flippant because they didn't think I could do it but it made me begin to explore. I didn't tell or discuss it with many people, but gradually others began to mention it to me and eventually I told my vicar.

At selection, when asked, 'Why do you want to be a Reader?' I could honestly answer, 'I don't want it but I feel it might be what God wants me to do so I need to explore it.' During training I always said, 'If I feel this isn't right I'll stop it. I don't want to be licensed to a ministry that God doesn't want me to do.' I've now been licensed for three years and I know that it has been the right thing.

## Carol – a Reader for one year

I was approached by an elderly Reader in the parish about ten years ago. I hadn't thought about Reader ministry and was about to train as a counsellor. My perceptions of Readers were different then and I found myself wondering, 'What does he see in me? How will I be able to stand up in the pulpit and speak?' The idea remained in the background and I became involved in some voluntary counselling work with bereaved people, with drug and alcohol users, and in a prison. Even though I wasn't sure that I was up to it academically, the idea of Reader ministry persisted. One thing led to another; I found myself in so many situations where people clearly wanted to become closer to God, and I found myself ministering to them. I took a break from voluntary coun-selling after six years to think things through. I didn't really know who to talk to at this time. Eventually I spoke very tentatively to my incumbent and I was gradually encouraged towards Reader ministry.

I wondered whether I'd be accepted because I'd had breast cancer some years earlier. It had come out of the blue and the prognosis was not good. The company had sent a chaplain to the house. I was devastated, but as I talked with the chaplain I realized that I had a real faith that was lying dormant; I felt there was something missing and went back to church. Thirteen years on I am in good health and have now completed my initial train-ing and been licensed as a Reader.

I've realized that it's about who you are as a person, not pre-senting yourself as what you think you ought to be. I felt that God was in the timing – I don't think he calls people to do things for which he doesn't equip them. Going back over my personal journey like this has been good and it's made me realize that there's been a lot of learning through all of this.

When you have finished reading all of these stories you might like to begin writing your own. Telling your story of vocation can often be helpful in trying to discern what you are being called to do.

## What do I do next?

If, having read this chapter and having reflected at length about your sense of calling, you feel called to explore Reader ministry further, your first course of action should be to approach your incumbent, who should have the details you need in order to pursue the matter further. The discernment process is likely to include a number of in-depth interviews that explore your calling; you can expect to be invited to share something of your personal story of faith, your prayer life and your engagement in the life of your church, as well as having an opportunity to say what you understand Reader min-istry to be about. The process by which people are recommended for training varies from one to diocese to another; in some dio-ceses selection interviews are arranged as and when required, while in other places they occur at regular intervals during the year or at one annual event. This means that you might need to wait for a little while for an interview date, but don't let this put you off applying. In every diocese the final arbiter concerning recommendation for training for all public ministry is the bishop.

# 5

# Formal study

## Introduction

When some people begin training they look forward to the practical accumulation of skills but dislike, and almost fear, the academic study of theology. Others lap up the academic study of theology and find the practical accumulation of skills unexciting and predictable. Between these two extremes are people who enjoy bits of different aspects, both academic and practical. The next two chapters explore the challenges of the academic study that you face and the issues of practical skills that Reader training will provide.

Of course, we need, even before we begin, to acknowledge that academic and practical are not quite as far apart as we might presume. For example, what could be more practical than learning to read the Bible carefully and well to enhance your sermons? Or what is more academic than engaging in a detailed sociological exploration of your local context? Academic study and the accumulation of practical skill go hand in hand in Reader training. Both are essential and equally important as you go forward into ministry. You may well tend toward one area more than the other, but it is good to engage with both as much as you can, since you need both areas to form firm foundations for your ministry.

## Engaging with academic study

### Facing your fears

A group of new Reader trainees were each given two sticky notes and asked to write on one what they were most looking forward to about training and on the other what they were most fearful or anxious about. The anonymous notes were then stuck onto a whiteboard and everyone had opportunity to read what the others had written. The hopes centred on getting to know scripture better, learning more about the Christian tradition, looking forward to learning the skills of ministry, becoming a good preacher or an effective pastor. The fears, almost without exception, were focused on the apprehension that they felt as they returned to academic work, sometimes after a gap of many years; especially acute were fears about writing essays and fear of failure.

Clearly people come with a wide range of different experiences, qualifications and abilities. Sometimes people's experience of school might have been quite negative: the school might not have served them well; they might have had little encouragement from home; they may be dyslexic or have another learning disability that may or may not have been diagnosed; they might just have had little interest at that stage of life in engaging with what was expected of them and 'switched off' from school. For others it is simply a long time since they have done any kind of formal education.

'Academic' is a word that is sometimes used to mean pedantic, abstract and irrelevant; some people also use the word 'theological' to mean the same thing. Academic theology, therefore, can sound distinctly uninspiring, but all it really means is 'talking about God in the context of serious study'. Study can be serious, purposeful and inspiring without being irrelevant or unintelligible.

One of the challenges about engaging in a serious study of faith and the Bible is the fact that it causes us to encounter new questions and to look again at many ideas that we have always taken for granted. Some people may tell you that theological study will harm your faith; we would sincerely hope that this will not be the case. Instead, you should find your faith stretched, challenged and expanded in more ways than you could possibly imagine at the start. This can only happen, however, if you approach your studies ready and willing for the task. Do not feel you need to defend God; God is more than capable of defending himself. In your ministry you will encounter and work with people with a wide range of theological ideas and you will need to be able to engage with them all. Ministers need to understand a range of theological perspectives, both those that are in line with their particular faith stance, and those that differ from it and that they themselves may not accept. In the marketplace of religious ideas that is twenty-first-century Britain, it is important for ministers to be able to address critiques of the Christian faith that are often presented in very articulate and persuasive ways. You can only do this if you have encountered and thought through these ideas in full.

One of the things that it is vital to bear in mind is that you are not alone. Here are some stories of people and their experiences of Reader training:

## Bob (trainee)

I left school at 14 with no qualifications and worked as a butcher until I was 18 when I joined the Army, where I went on to become a master butcher. I trained as an armed explosives dog handler too. While in the Army I did various courses of Christian education. At first, the study required for Reader training was very difficult for me – learning to use a computer and writing essays. A lot of the terms were new and I sometimes felt out of my depth. But overall it's been very exciting. I thought I'd read the Bible until I did this course and discovered that I'd only really flicked through it.

It's given me a better understanding of my faith and of other people's faith – and I'm really enjoying it. I've now finished two years of study at Level One and I really think that Level Two would be too difficult. I've had some ill health and fallen behind a bit, so my tutor and I have decided that although I'll attend the Level Two modules I won't submit any more written work. When I started out I wanted to be a Reader to work with people in the parish – it wasn't about getting a qualification. I've had one-to-one help with a tutor arranged by the course and lots of tips and support. There's no point sitting back and worrying that you can't do it. Pluck up the courage to ask for help. If you need help you need to step up to the plate and say so.

## Dianne (Reader)

I was quite nervous about going back to study. It was good to get stuck into it and begin to look at things I didn't know or didn't understand. The course wasn't just heavily academic; I never felt as though I was being told, 'Swallow these chunks of information'! I developed enormously during my time in training. From a personal perspective it was really important for me, even though it was sometimes hard to keep going. It's had a knock-on effect on my life. I grew in confidence as a person. To begin with I felt uncomfortable in the classroom – I felt that I was not adequate for the task God had called me to do. It was getting over this with the help of others that enabled me to go on and be where I am now. The thought of standing in a pulpit was the biggest thing I had to overcome. I now enjoy it even though I still feel nervous. There's no point learning things and leaving them in the computer for your next ten years in ministry – what you learn is relevant and, although you don't quote it, the learning is useful in ministry.

Anxieties are not just limited to those who have not studied for a while or who struggled while at school. People who have studied on previous courses can sometimes feel apprehensive too, and this can include those whose professional lives are spent in an academic environment as teachers in schools or universities. Being in a different role can bring its own insecurities regardless of experience or ability. Saying this is not intended to make you feel anxious or to fear the course that lies ahead, but to reassure you. Others have been in the same situation as you and others on your course will also be feeling nervous (even if they are trying not to show it). Before you know where you are, things will begin to fall into place, relationships will be established and the first piece of work will have been submitted – and hopefully passed.

It is important, however, to share your anxieties if you can, either with your tutor or with your fellow students. The vast majority of the time your fears will be shared by most other people on your course and represent a natural anxiety about starting something new. Very occasionally they represent some real issues that need addressing. These will not prevent you doing the course, but the sooner you get one-to-one help the sooner you will be able to move beyond them and take a full part in the course and all it holds.

### Ian (Reader)

When I was in the RAF I did an Open University degree in maths and computer science, so I had a BSc and was used to part-time study – though it had been some years previously. I've enjoyed the academic side of training and I think it's absolutely vital. If you are to communicate the Christian story effectively then you need to have a reasonably thorough grasp of theology, otherwise you can't speak with authority. As well as Reader trainees and others who had a ministerial interest in study there were a few undergraduates on my course, so the age range was late teens to 60-plus. The unifying bond was the great sense of fellowship. People were taking these modules in the main because of the love of Christ. We had an excellent rapport within the group and the tutors covered the subjects with both academic rigour and theological sensitivity. We covered the sorts of subjects that I had expected, but in greater depth than I'd anticipated. This gave me a greater understanding of my theological base, opened my eyes to a range of issues I'd never thought of before and encouraged me to be better read. I feel that I can now speak with confidence when I'm trying to put something across.

There's been some controversy about the way that Reader training has evolved. A number of people have said that it's far too academic. I don't believe that. You need to have a thorough grounding in theology and ministry if you're going to be an effective lay theologian and minister. There's no point if asked a question saying, 'Sorry, we never covered that.' You need to have sufficient basic knowledge, and the tools available to be able to identify the sources to call upon to do justice to the people you're ministering among. You also need to be able to see both sides of an argument. Without this you'd be swimming in a very shallow sea and would soon flounder.

## Stewart (trainee)

I've just completed my first year of Reader training and it's been a challenge. It's moved me out of my comfort zone. So far we've studied the Old Testament, Christian ethics and mission and ministry. It's gone into a greater depth than I expected. I'd been away from study for a long time. The first assignment was a huge shock – I felt as though I was swimming in treacle. There's a word limit for our assignments and I found that all my research branched out wider and wider. I had to be really discerning about what were the important points to make and what to discard, and I'd got out of that routine – though I somehow managed to get a B for the assignment – I don't know how. Having other students in the same boat and being able to discuss it together helps you to sharpen up your thoughts – and where your thoughts conflict with other people's you realize that you've got to start making your argument concrete and precise. I know that the tutors are there to help, and as the year's worn on and I've got to know them I've felt it easier to ask for help. Being part of a mixed group of students with a wide variety of backgrounds – not just church, but life and social backgrounds – has been a privilege. It's been useful to be able to share ideas and exchange similar difficulties – we've been able to help each other.

The range of approaches that tutors have used has been extremely varied. There have been lectures, PowerPoint presentations, and class and group discussions. Sometimes – for example with ethics – you think, 'Ah, I've got it', only to find that like a bar of soap it's slipped out of your hands. Student presentations have been helpful; there's no element of being competitive, we've had to learn to work together and support each other, and we get a lot out of it.

## Why do I need to be trained?

So we can see that returning to study after a break of some years can feel like a very daunting undertaking. Sometimes people say, 'I already do so much in my parish, why won't the Church just license me as a Reader – why do I need to do all this training?' Training is important. Being a committed disciple of Jesus, a pillar of your local church and a kind and caring person to all whom you meet is a good place to start, but these on their own won't be sufficient to equip you for a public, authorized ministry in the Church.

If you are going to be representing the Church in preaching, teaching and pastoral care, it is important that you have at least some knowledge of certain important theological issues. Once you are licensed it is likely that some people at least will want to talk to you about deep and complex theological questions, such as why God allows suffering, what happens after you die, whether euthanasia is ethical or not. Of course, your training will not provide you with pre-packaged answers to every difficult question, but it will begin to train you in where to begin, how to think your way into an answer, what Christians have said throughout Christian history, and so on. Your training will provide you with the building blocks of ministerial formation. Do not expect that you will know everything – or even most things – that you will need to know by the time you complete your pre-licensing training. What your training aims to do is to set you on the path of a lifelong journey of exploration. It teaches you how to ask the questions you will need to fuel your preaching, teaching and pastoral care for many years to come.

As you go through your training you may sometimes struggle to see the relevance of some aspects of the academic work that you're required to undertake, and when this happens you may simply need to take it on trust that every part of it has a purpose. In time, once you embark upon your Reader ministry, the point of much of it will become clear. This might sound a bit like 'Jam yesterday, jam tomorrow but never jam today'; rest assured that there will be enough in the theology you study to enthuse you and make it seem rather more appealing than simply a means to an end. It's the experience of the vast majority of Reader trainees that training provides plenty of jam today too – and more than enough to go around!

## What will the teaching be like?

Throughout the course you will be given the opportunity to engage in a variety of ways. Some taught sessions will contain more formal input than others, but it will be a clear expectation of your course that all participants attend on a regular basis, that they engage in discussion, that they complete the required preparation between sessions (which may be some reading or a small amount of field work), and that they complete the work set for formal assessment. The assessment strategies will vary; they may include any or all of the following:

- essay
- exegesis
- reflective journal
- individual and group presentation
- preparing and leading worship (perhaps in small groups)

- planning a Lent course
- planning a children's activity day
- recording a 'Thought for the Day'.

You will learn more about the detail of this once you have embarked upon your course.

It is essential you make every effort to keep strictly to the time-table given for the completion of your work. The deadlines have not been created in order to inconvenience you or to make your life difficult, but because missing one deadline can easily lead to the missing of the next as the work backs up. There is nothing that makes students more disheartened than the feeling that it is all 'running away with them' and that they will never be able to catch up!

One particularly positive feature of studying on most Reader training programmes is that they will give you the opportunity to meet with other people who are engaged either in Reader training along-side you, or in other forms of ministerial education, or in further-ing their own theological knowledge as independent students. Each group of students is very mixed: many will already be graduates or postgraduates or have qualifications in their chosen fields, while others will have left school with no formal qualifications. This diver-sity within the student body is one of the greatest strengths of the training period, and students regularly say how much they value the opportunity to share experiences and thoughts with others. So, as we have said, be reassured – if you are beginning study and are aware that other people in your group have more by way of formal academic qualifications than you, do not be overawed. Those people may well be having difficulty adjusting to a very different subject from the one with which they are already familiar. Through the study you are undertaking, you yourself will be helped to reach your potential as a theological thinker. You will have the opportu-nity to contribute important experiences and profound insights – and remember, profound does not mean 'expressed in fancy words and long sentences'.

The development of Regional Training Partnerships within the Church of England has increased the amount of co-operation and sharing of resources that exists between dioceses with regard to Reader (and other theological) training, but although it is no longer the case that each diocese runs a completely separate and distinct course, neither is there one single 'blueprint' for Reader training that all must adopt. The Church of England's publication *Shaping the Future* sets out the areas of study that Reader trainees will be expected to cover. At the stage of initial training these are (in brief):

- scripture – and its relevance in the world today;
- Christian doctrine – in the history of the Church and with regard to its Anglican emphases;
- worship – understanding its theology and learning to lead it;
- mission – ways in which the Church might engage with those outside itself;
- moral, ethical and social justice issues – learning to reflect theologically on life's challenges;
- preaching – proclaiming Christ with confidence in a range of contexts;
- pastoral skills – listening, encouraging, nurturing, etc.;
- spirituality – an understanding of the tradition and the growth of personal prayer, commitment and discipleship;
- communication skills – including an understanding of learning styles, collaborative skills and evaluative skills.

The Church also expects that Readers will have some understanding of appropriate ways of working with children and young people and will be aware of the legislation governing this area of its life.

## A word about buying books

A recommendation for training for ministry can sometimes lead people to embark on an enthusiastic book-buying spending spree. Be very cautious about buying too many books before your training starts unless you are very sure of what you are doing. Theology books (like books for most academic subjects) can be very expensive and you could easily run up a large bill acquiring things that prove not to be much use in the long run. Take advice wherever possible. Be especially cautious about buying books on the internet; this can be a good way of saving money if you are sure of what you need but a poor way to make a choice if you aren't so sure, as you can't browse through the books as you can in a shop. Your Reader training programme will have provision for access to a library; it might be best to wait until you have seen what is available and then supplement this with a few books that you are likely to be able to use more than once.

# 6

# Developing practical skills

## Introduction

Sometimes, as Reader trainees approach their admission and licensing, they experience an increasing lack of confidence about whether they can do it or not. In the words of one trainee a week or so before the licensing service, 'But I don't know everything yet, I might be asked to do something that I've not done before, or that I've not practised enough!' If you feel like this, it is important to recognize that you are not alone. Many people feel like this as they face the realization that they are soon to be called upon to practise that ministry to which they have felt called for so long. It is also a very healthy sign of your own levels of self-awareness. It would be much more troubling if you felt that you knew everything you need to know about Reader ministry before you even began.

Following Jesus involves us constantly being stretched and drawn beyond what we feel we can do. Part of our calling as ministers (in fact, as disciples of Jesus generally) is to be fresh, life-giving streams of water. Flowing water is fresh and life-giving, whereas pools of water that have no in-flow or out-flow quickly become stagnant. It is a part of human nature that as soon as we feel confident in our abilities about something we stop trying so hard, so we need to develop an attitude of mind that is prepared to look onwards and outwards to what God might be saying to the Church right now and to face new challenges with courage. In short, if as you approach your licensing you feel anxious about whether you can do it, you are already embracing this way of life. Hold onto this feeling, as it is this that will enable you to grow throughout your ministry into the person that God longs for you to be.

## Placements and your local church

There will be opportunities to engage with a range of practical aspects of Reader ministry during your training, though the detail of how these are organized will differ from diocese to diocese. Almost all trainees undertake at least one placement as part of the overall training programme in a different parish or another ministerial context and you will be encouraged to reflect theologically upon the ministry that you encounter there and upon the tasks that you engage with. Most trainee Readers are eager for their placement to begin, as they imagine that this is where the greater part of their learning will take place.

It may be, however, that before you embark on a placement elsewhere you will be asked to study your own church – to stand back and look at it through different, perhaps more objective, eyes. This can sometimes leave people feeling short-changed; they want to 'get out there' and start the 'real business' of learning the skills of Reader ministry. Although being on placement in a parish different from your own can have huge benefits, taking this time to look in detail at your own context – whether or not it's a formal part of your training programme – can be invaluable.

It helps you to raise important questions, such as:

- What do we do in our church? Why do we do things this way?
- What is our strategy for mission?
- How do we ensure that those on the margins are welcomed?
- How does our church welcome newcomers and those who are unfamiliar with what happens here (including people of different ages)?
- What impact does our local situation have on our church and its ministry?
- Why do we worship in this way?

Many Reader trainees have discovered that there can be great value in asking such questions in and of their home parish, and very often the church community as a whole (and not just the Reader trainee) says how much they have benefited from walking alongside someone who is stopping, looking, questioning and reflecting. Whether your particular training course requires you to evaluate your own context or not, you might find it valuable to ask these questions informally in order to help you to begin to see your own church slightly more from the outside.

## On being reflective practitioners

One of the purposes both of your placement and of the reflection upon your own local context is to encourage you to become 'reflective practitioners'. There's an often-quoted line in one of T. S. Eliot's *Four Quartets*, a set of four poems about time and our relationship to it, which runs, 'We had the experience but missed the meaning.' For many people this perhaps sums up much of life for much of the time. We can be so busy getting on with all that needs to be done, fitting everything into the day, keeping several balls in the air at the same time – or perhaps just sticking without much further thought to the routine that we've developed over the years – that we don't always pay a great deal of attention to what lies beneath the surface of our life's activity. Training for ministry means that we need to develop some new skills in order that we can learn to look at things more deeply; we need to have strategies for searching for meaning and we need to develop ways of interpreting life in the light of God's ongoing creative presence within, and redeeming love for, the world. In order that we might do this effectively we need to:

- have an informed and intelligent understanding of scripture;
- be familiar with the beliefs and traditions of the Church;
- develop the capacity to slow down so that we have sufficient time to see properly . . . and . . .
- stand back in order that our seeing might be as objective as possible;
- be open to the importance of context and learn how to interpret it;
- be willing to accept that our dearly held views might be just that;
- be open to change in ourselves and in our way of assessing situations;
- be alert to the reality of God's involvement in every event and circumstance;
- work collaboratively wherever possible.

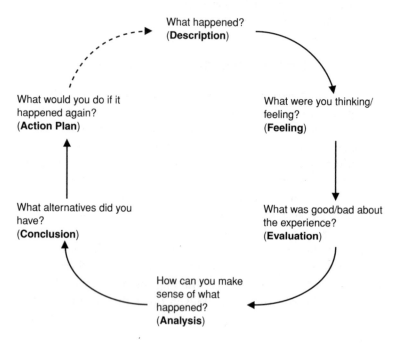

**Figure 6.1 The cycle of reflective practice[3]**

Reflective practice is used in many settings, such as nursing or teaching, as well as in the Church. It is based on a cycle of acting, reflecting and analysing. The idea is that you become skilled at observing what you do, reflect on what was good, ask about what needs changing and then put what you have learned into action.

There are numerous ways of describing the cycle of reflective practice but one of the most helpful for many people is shown in Figure 6.1. The reason why this is called a cycle is that whatever lessons you learn from these questions are taken into the next thing that you do, using your experience and your reflection upon that experience to transform how you act next.

Theological reflection is like reflective practice but is shaped to reflect specifically theological questions and issues. In recent years a generic framework has been developed for 'doing' theological reflection. The detail varies from one expression of it to another but the basic structure is as follows:

- Identify a particular situation or circumstance and describe it, asking 'What?' questions such as:
  - What happened? . . . or . . .
  - What did you do? . . . or . . .
  - What did others do?
  - What is the context of the event or occurrence that you have chosen?
  - Or whatever other describing questions are appropriate in the context.
- Now consider some 'Why?' and 'Who?' questions:
  - Why did things work out like this? . . . or . . .
  - Why did things come to be like this? . . . or . . .
  - Who is instrumental here? . . . or . . .
  - Who holds the power/has the capacity for influence etc.?
- How does the Christian tradition speak into this situation? Reflect on:
  - Where is God in this?
  - What bearing does scripture have on the situation?
  - What can we learn from the Church's history and beliefs?
  - What can you bring from your own experience and that of others?
  - What is your observation of the event in its context?
- Now ask the all-important 'So what?' questions:
  - What difference has your reflection made?
  - How might you (or others) react or respond differently next time?
  - Are there any conclusions that you can come to, even if they are tentative ones?
  - Is there anything else that needs to be done to get a better outcome either now or in the future?
- Having reached this point in the process of theological reflection, why not pause for a moment to review the process prayerfully, committing it to God and leaving with God any difficult or painful feelings or emotions that have arisen in the course of your reflection?

Remember in all of this that theological reflection is a way of ensuring that your ministry is God-shaped and your life is God-filled. It's a way of finding meaning in the many events, simple and complex, that make up life; it isn't just about finding a mechanistic way of solving problems. The framework given above is just a guide; there can be no one-size-fits-all blueprint for reflecting theologically as every situation is unique and will require its own approach. What the framework does is set out the sort of way in which theological reflection can be undertaken, and from this you can work out your own way of doing it as each individual situation demands.

People sometimes turn up their noses at the idea of theological reflection or regard it as something of a Cinderella aspect of theology. It *is* real theology, because it draws on the Bible and Christian insights about God's relation with us and his world; but at the same time it need not have any great mystique attached to it. In many ways it's simply an extended version of what we do all the time as we think about God's involvement in human lives – but, as we noted above, this sometimes gets squeezed out in our eagerness to finish one thing and move on to the next, so having a framework can help.

## Recording your practical experience

Alongside the notes that you keep as part of the reflective practice cycle, it can also be helpful to develop the practice of keeping a careful record of your engagement with the practical aspects of training (and indeed of your ministry as a whole), not just as a list of what you've done but as a means of reflecting on the experience. Your training programme may require or encourage this, but whether or not it is a formal part of your training it can be a useful exercise and one that can help you to track your progress throughout your time of training. It will probably be possible for you to undertake some of these practical elements in your home parish as well as in placement and perhaps other locations.

To help you with this, here is a suggestion for keeping a brief record of the things you are engaged in. (See Figure 6.2. It is easy for you to produce this, or something similar, on a computer and copy it as required.) You will see that there are only small spaces provided for noting factual information: what, where and when, as well as a little space for you to record your personal, theological reflection. There is also room for the comments of someone else – perhaps your supervisor or a member of the group or congregation you were working with – by way of feedback. The form is

| |
|---|
| Date                          Venue |
| Activity engaged in/task undertaken/event |
| Reflection |
| Feedback from others |

**Figure 6.2  Recording and reflecting on activities**

intentionally short; it can be trickier to say something meaningful in a few words than it can to write reams of unfocused thoughts. This is not complex! It is merely a simple way of taking a disciplined approach to something that can easily be left in the 'good intentions' part of our brain.

Those responsible for Reader training in the Church recognize that trainees' prior experience in leading worship, preaching, pastoral work and other related activities varies tremendously from one person to another. What follows, therefore, is not intended as a slavish register of every single lesson read or prayer prayed. Rather, it provides an opportunity for you to think in particular about those aspects of ministry that are new to you or in which you have no previous experience, and to build on those areas in which you already have a degree of competence.

## Leading worship – an introduction

Leading worship is one of the great privileges of ministry. As you settle into training you will gradually begin to take part in leading worship that is formal, informal, liturgical, experimental, traditional, contemporary and so on, depending upon your situation. You have perhaps been looking forward with equal amounts of eagerness and trepidation to the day when you begin to lead worship. You have prepared well; you know which parts of the service you will be leading and there is someone experienced with you. And then what . . . ?

It's not uncommon for people to say that they didn't expect to encounter any real difficulties in leading worship; they were familiar with the liturgy of the Church of England, either from *Common Worship* or the Book of Common Prayer and knew the services like the back of their hand. But when they stood up to help lead worship for the first time it felt very different all of a sudden being 'up front' rather than sitting in the congregation.

- Do we sing a hymn now?
- What comes next?
- Why don't I feel as though I'm in control of this when I know it so well and have prepared so carefully?
- Why do I need to focus so much of my energy on leading worship for others that I really struggle to engage in worship myself at the same time?

- How do I handle all the books and bits of paper?
- Where should I be now, and should I be sitting or standing?
- Help – what do I do if I think I've made a mistake?

It might sound strange, but this is an experience common to very many people in the early (and not so early!) stages. So if this is you – be reassured that you are not alone. Gradually you will begin to feel more confident and you will learn to be able to worship at the same time as leading worship for others. In the meantime remember that learning to lead others is, for now, your offering to God in the time and at the place in which you find yourself, and God will accept that as your contribution to worship. Above all, never lose sight of the fact, at any stage of your ministry, that the reason we engage in worship is that God might be glorified. Yes, it's honouring to God that we prepare carefully, but God will still be glorified if we occasionally mess up. If we 'beat ourselves up' every time something is not perfect then we are perhaps embracing a distorted view of God, of worship, of ourselves or of any combination of these. So, why not file away this unassailable truth in the back of your mind somewhere for when the day comes that you need to remind yourself of it? *God calls us both to discipleship and to ministry, accepts us as we are and takes the risk that we won't always get it right. We don't somehow have to make ourselves and our ministry perfect before they become acceptable.*

Let's give some thought, then, to some of the different aspects of Reader ministry for which training will begin to equip you.

## Morning/Evening Prayer

It will be important that you gain some experience in leading Morning and/or Evening Prayer, and, preferably, that you are familiar with the traditions of both the Book of Common Prayer (where the services are also called Matins and Evensong) and *Common Worship*. You'll need to be aware of the layout of the different service books in which these offices are to be found and to be able to find your way around the Revised Common Lectionary (the set readings for each Sunday and major festival) as used by the Church of England. (This will be useful even if your own church does not use the lectionary as there may be occasions when you are asked to plan collaborative services with churches who do use the lectionary or be invited to preach in a church that does.) In some churches there will be an expectation that you don't deviate in any way from the book. In other places you can be a little freer or more relaxed; but be careful here – most people who attend Morning or Evening Prayer (as opposed to morning or evening worship or something with a similar title) come because they love the words of the service and its constant, formal, almost unchanging character. Your task in leading such worship is that you allow and even encourage people to engage for themselves with the words of the service. If you do your job well people will barely notice it is you!

## Informal worship

The opportunities for leading informal worship will vary tremendously from one person to the next. For some Reader trainees this will be the normal pattern in their home church, while for others it will be quite new. Informal worship comes in many styles and shapes and forms. Some churches have a much freer style of worship than others. Before taking part in leading any informal worship you will need to observe it as it happens in your particular context, and you'll need to talk with those responsible for worship so that you can gain some sense of the overall approach taken in the parish. You may be required, as your confidence grows, to take responsibility for devising an entire act of worship, though this could be something as simple as a ten-minute reflective service during Holy Week, or as complex as an all-age service in a busy church on a Sunday.

Probably the most important thing to remember is that that 'informal worship' does not mean 'unplanned worship'. The best informal worship services can take around four times as much time to plan as the formal ones.

## Assisting in the leading of eucharistic worship

Most services of Holy Communion according to the BCP rite are likely to be led entirely by the priest, except for reading lessons and administering Holy Communion.

With *Common Worship* there are opportunities for an assisting minister to take a role in leading the worship (see *Common Worship: Services and Prayers*, p. 158), though in some contexts the president (or leader of the service) will still lead the service throughout. As a Reader trainee you will need to gain experience in assisting in the leading of eucharistic worship according to the *Common Worship* rites. Remember, though, that customs differ from one church to another, so although you will need to know how to do this (since Readers may visit other parishes or even transfer their licence to another parish) it may be that it isn't the practice in your local church. Reader training, however, is designed to train you for ministry both in your own context and beyond it.

## Administering Holy Communion

The Reader has a key role in assisting in the administration of Holy Communion. There are a number of contexts in which this takes place: within worship in a church building; in old people's homes and similar venues; in hospital (though in practice this is generally undertaken by the hospital chaplain); and with individuals or small groups in the homes of people who are unable to attend church.

When administering Communion in church, the usual pattern of that church will be followed. In other venues it will be important to give due consideration to such matters as length and form of service, appropriate dress and such simple but important matters as washing one's hands before and after giving people Communion and the reverent handling of consecrated elements.

It is also helpful to learn the words of administration, including the longer form in the Book of Common Prayer, which you may be expected to know in some contexts, so that you can say them clearly and without stumbling (e.g. 'The Body of Christ keep you in eternal life', and 'The Body of our Lord Jesus Christ which was given for thee preserve thy body and soul unto everlasting life. Take and eat this in remembrance that Christ died for thee, and feed on him in thy heart by faith with thanksgiving.'). People who have hearing difficulties may be helped by being able to watch your lips as you say them – so form the words clearly, even if you speak quietly. Don't be afraid to ask for as much training or practice as you feel you need in order to administer Communion confidently.

## Leading intercessions

Intercession forms part of most acts of public worship. It is an opportunity for the Church to hold particular people, places and situations before God and to seek God's will and purpose for them. Intercession is not about persuading God to bring about a particular outcome or do what we think would be best in any given situation. In all our intercession God is there before us: we are not informing God or presenting him with lists or instructions. Some years ago a person (now long dead) in a certain parish used to lead the intercessions during the Eucharist like this:

> Dear God, we pray for the Parish Council meeting that will take place at 7.30 p.m. in the Town Hall on Wednesday – to which you are all invited. We pray for the matters being discussed: fencing the children's play area; parking and litter. We ask you, Lord, to bless us, and we hope to see as many of you attend as possible.

There was clearly some confusion here between intercession and a bulletin board!

When leading intercessions it is important that you address biddings to the congregation ('Let us pray for . . .') but prayers to God ('Most gracious God, we pray . . .'). As well as rejoicing in the world there is much for us to grieve over; remember to include the world and not just the church and church community in your prayers. Give them a clear structure so that people know what's going on and try to ensure that your intercessions don't fall into a pattern that you simply repeat every time you lead them. Most importantly of all, avoid giving out notices in your prayers. If there is something about which you need to pray (the death of a loved member of the congregation; meetings taking place in the week) then ensure that the congregation knows about this in advance. It is very hard to pray properly for something if it is coming as news to you during the prayers.

## Teaching/leading groups

Teaching covers a wide range of areas, such as baptism preparation, confirmation preparation, leading Bible studies, home groups and prayer groups. It's an area of Reader ministry that people often find quite daunting, either because they feel that they have no previous experience in engaging in this sort of activity in a leadership role, or because they have experience of specific sorts of teaching (for example in a school or a university), and discover that the skills required for teaching within the parish are in many ways quite different from those that they already possess. For example, it would clearly be inappropriate for someone used to teaching 7-year-olds to lead an adult Bible study group in the same style that they would use for children. It will be important during the course of your training to take the opportunities that are afforded by your placements and other contexts to observe experienced ministers in these activities in order that you might develop or build upon your own skills and abilities.

This teaching aspect of Reader ministry means that you will need to look at what might be involved in teaching adults, but even more importantly it will help you to appreciate the different ways in which people learn. If this is completely new to you, take a look (there's plenty on the internet) at David A. Kolb's work on learning styles or at Peter Honey and Alan Mumford's development of this. You might discover something about your own ways of thinking and learning, too.

# The Reader as pastor

Although Reader ministry is generally described primarily as being a preaching and teaching ministry, pastoral work is an essential component of Reader ministry. This includes such areas as visiting members of the church; visiting the people who either have never come to church or who have left at some point in the past; visiting the sick at home, in care homes and in hospital; bereavement visiting, or general visiting by request. Initially Reader trainees will accompany a priest or an experienced Reader when undertaking visits. It will be important to bear in mind such things as timing of visits (no one wants to have their meals interrupted, no matter how worthy your intentions); sensitivity in gauging appropriate visiting hours (preferably in daylight unless the visit is pre-arranged); due caution with regard to visiting people in their homes on their own (it is important that your own good intentions are not open to misinterpretation, or worse, compromised by someone with a different agenda). You will need to be discerning when it comes to recording anything connected with pastoral work; it is *essential* that you do not record personal details of a confidential nature about anybody at all or write in such a way that individuals can be identified.

Here is a little cautionary tale:

Jane was a brand new Reader. Shortly after her licensing she noticed someone new in the congregation. At the end of the service the woman, Sarah, approached Jane. 'Are you a minister here? I need to talk with someone,' she said. Jane felt a little puff of pride. All those years of training and here she was, part of the ministry team of the parish. Already, just two weeks in, her pastoral skills were being called upon. Jane talked to Sarah over coffee and as she left Sarah said how very helpful their conversation had been. The following week Sarah approached Jane again and they talked for twenty minutes or so. Jane began to realize that for a second week she had hardly spoken to anyone else. When Sarah again said how good it was that she could talk to Jane so freely, Jane suggested that they meet during the week when there would be more time, and more privacy, for their conversation. A pattern developed and Sarah regularly spoke to Jane about things that were worrying her: burdens long carried and fears for the future; a sense of hopelessness about how hard she found life; an acknowledgement that she had always felt rejected by others – but that with Jane to talk to she was sure that things would soon start to pick up.

Sarah sought more and more of Jane's time and began phoning her regularly in the evenings. Jane slowly began to realize that all was not well. She had felt flattered that someone had sought her out as a pastor, but things were beginning to get a bit out of hand. How had she got into this situation? Jane realized that she needed to pull back. She talked things through with Peter, her vicar, and they decided that next time they would see Sarah together and help her to make contact with a professional counsellor who would have the training and expertise to help her address the many deep-seated problems that she had been rehearsing with Jane week after week. The meeting seemed to go well enough and Jane felt a huge sense of relief when Sarah appeared to be happy to be referred to a counsellor. They said that they were looking forward to seeing her in church on Sunday and suggested that she might join a fellowship group and get to know a few more people in the church.

A few days later a card was pushed through Jane's letterbox. 'I won't be coming to church any more,' it read. 'I thought you were different, but now you've ended up rejecting me too – just like all the others. It's been the story of my life. I wish I'd never met you. Goodbye.' Jane realized that she'd helped to repeat the cycle of rejection that Sarah had spent so long describing to her as she'd spoken about her life.

It's so easy to see how Jane got herself caught up in this situation: she was new to ministry; she was sought out by someone who needed help; she jumped in with both feet, keen to be a listening ear to someone in distress; but eventually she began to feel trapped by the situation and she needed help to bail out.

It will be important as you begin to take on more and more pastoral work that you are alert to how much the need to be needed can accompany our offering for ministry. There is nothing dishonourable about this, it comes as part of the human condition, but you need to be able to articulate it and to recognize the symptoms before you get into situations that might prove to be difficult both for you and for others. Similarly, it's important for your pastoral visits not to stray too much into the area of giving advice or counselling. If conversations get into areas where you feel uncomfortable or out of your depth, it is appropriate for you to bring it to an end and help the person involved seek appropriate help from qualified professionals.

## Leading funerals

Canon E4 2A states:

> The Bishop may authorise a Reader to bury the dead or read the burial service before, at or after a cremation but only, in each case, with the goodwill of the persons responsible and at the invitation of the minister.

It is becoming increasingly common for Readers to share in the taking of funerals in their parishes and this significant piece of work is one for which careful training, preparation and supervision are essential. It would be exceptional for a Reader trainee to take a funeral on his or her own. You will need to discuss with your incumbent the extent to which you are likely to be involved in this ministry once you are admitted and licensed, and to ensure that you have proper one-to-one training in this according to local circumstances and tradition. Some dioceses include training on leading funerals during initial training, while many others provide post-licensing training sessions for Readers who are already exercising a ministry.

As a general rule, even when licensed, Readers do not accept direct requests or invitations, either from families or undertakers, to conduct funerals. All requests generally come from the incumbent or rural/area dean unless other, specific arrangements have been agreed. It is usual for a statutory minister's fee to be payable in respect of the funeral of an adult. Such fees contribute to the incumbent's fixed stipend – or, in practice, to the stipends budget in the diocese. You will need to check on local practice as decided upon by your diocese, but it would be exceptional for a fee to be retained by the Reader personally, and the assumption ought to be that any money handed to you personally will be given to your incumbent or treasurer in order that it might be assigned to the diocese.

Whether or not you actually take part in conducting funerals, it is highly likely that you will encounter people who have been bereaved. You will address this as part of your training programme.

## Preaching

Preaching the gospel is a privileged aspect of public ministry, and developing confidence in preaching will be an important part of your formation as a Reader. Remember that even the most accomplished preachers quite probably felt over-awed by the task when they first set out. There was a first time for everyone. It is not expected that you will be a skilled preacher from your very first sermon; there are many skills to be learnt in both the writing and delivery of sermons, some of which can only be developed by hands-on experience.

In the early days of his ministry Tom was struggling to write a sermon. His wife Susie was in the next room and she could hear his occasional thump on the table; things were clearly not going well. Sometimes Tom's sermons seem to fly through his fingers and on to the page but today it was proving to be rather a struggle. Susie couldn't decide whether asking how things were going would help or make matters worse, but eventually she popped her head round the door. 'I've spent for ever working on this but I just can't get it to take shape.' Tom's voice was filled with frustration. He asked Susie to read through what he'd written. 'Where are you trying to get to?' she asked a few moments later. 'The bottom of page four!' Tom exclaimed.

Many preachers will be able to think back to their early days and empathize with this. What do we want to say? (Or what do we believe God wants us to say?) How are we going to say it? Have we started thinking about it soon enough? Have we allocated too little time to the task, or have we set aside so much time that the lack of a sense of urgency is hampering our thinking? Be reassured that although there is no short-cut here, most preachers eventually find that with practice their ideas flow more readily and that the tasks both of writing and of delivering sermons gradually take on a better sense of proportion – at least most of the time!

Some trainee Readers will have vast previous experience in teaching, lecturing or other forms of speaking in public, but it is essential that preaching is understood as a quite distinct genre. Although some skills can be readily transferred, there will be many new things that have to be learnt – and perhaps some that have to be unlearnt too. Preaching is a complex combination of teaching, the unfolding of scripture, practical and personal application. Most of all it is the proclamation of the Word of God in this moment and to this congregation. Each one of these elements is important:

- proclaiming (not talking about but speaking forth);
- the Word of God (both from the scriptures and of the presence of Jesus – the Word made flesh);
- in this moment (and not any other – which is why repeated sermons rarely work);
- to this congregation (the best sermons are often given by someone who knows the gathered people of God well).

It is also important to add to all of these elements, the unique gifts and personality of the person preaching. One of the most important lessons in preaching is to discover your own voice. Trying to imitate the style of someone else will never be successful. Take the best of what you see in other people's sermons, but weave it together with your own experience and skills to find your own God-given style of preaching.

In order to achieve this you will find feedback from others vitally important throughout your years of ministry as a Reader, but never more so than in the early stages when you are developing your own individual style and approach. Your preaching will be evaluated by others during the course of your training so that you can receive feedback on the style, content and delivery of your sermons. Try to listen to what is being said, even if you do not always instinctively agree with it; the comments made about us by others that we find hardest to hear are sometimes those that contain the most truth. Gradually you will develop your own style and find your own voice.

As you engage with the task of preaching you may meet two technical words that you will need to be familiar with: *hermeneutics* and *homiletics*. Hermeneutics is concerned with the interpretation of the text of scripture, not only in its own context but for today as well. Homiletics is the art of preaching and focuses on the writing and delivery of sermons. These two distinct but related areas of theology are worth investigating as you prepare to begin preaching. Try to keep them in mind when you hear others preach and see if you can begin to identify the hermeneutical and homiletical approaches that they take.

You might find it helpful to do some reading around the area of preaching. In your course you will be given some good and helpful reading lists which will probably include books on preaching, but Day (2004) and Stevenson and Wright (2008) are very helpful. Publication details are in the 'References and further reading' section at the end of this book.

## Feedback on preaching

It is important that you receive feedback on your preaching, and as there should ideally be a licensed minister present when you preach as a Reader trainee he or she would be well placed to evaluate your sermon. You might also like to ask other members of the ministry team, or a churchwarden or another member of the congregation. It's good if feedback can be given soon after the event while it's fresh in people's minds – and without the preacher being kept wondering what the response will be. If feedback is to be constructive it really needs to be honestly (but kindly) expressed. It can be tempting only to want to hear 'nice things' said, but, in the longer term, bland or uncritical comment does not help people develop as preachers. 'Was that all right?' might get a bland reply; 'Tell me two things I could have done better' will more probably elicit something useful. Of course, if being assessed on your preaching seems rather daunting, you could always suggest that other members of the ministry team, including perhaps the vicar, allow others to evaluate their preaching too!

## All ministers remain works in progress

At the end of your initial training, when you will be admitted and licensed as a Reader, you will embark upon a fledgling public ministry in which you will still need regular support from others, lots of advice and someone to talk to when you feel out of your depth, or when you find yourself in a situation that is new or unnerving. A crucial aim of the training period is that by the time you become a Reader, you should be feeling sure enough to begin to engage with a range of aspects of ministry with some degree of confidence – at least on the outside, even if you feel inwardly that you are still paddling like crazy beneath the surface. You will have been given opportunities to practise leading worship and will have begun to preach and to dip your toes in the sorts of things that Readers do. If you can do this in a way that enhances the experience of others then you have reached the stage at which the Church can launch you into ministry with confidence.

It cannot be stressed too strongly that all ministers, at whatever stage of their training or ministry, remain 'works in progress'. There are always new skills to be learned and old skills to be developed further. Initial training provides the basic building blocks that you will need in your Reader ministry; you will have the rest of your life to improve them and hone them.

You might find it useful to read the Church of England's booklet *Guidelines for the Professional Conduct of the Clergy* (2003), which, although written for the guidance of the clergy, contains much advice that, together with a theological rationale, is also relevant to and helpful for Readers.

# 7

# Spirituality and formation
# for ministry

It goes without saying that all those seeking to engage in ministry will be people with a lively relationship with God – women and men of faith and prayer and commitment. Academic study of theology, and learning the practical skills for ministry, will have an impact upon this side of a minister's (or trainee minister's) life.

Earlier we gave some thought to the Church of England's selection criteria for Reader ministry and we saw that these work in two ways:

- They help the *Church* to know what it is looking for in its ministers and to discern a calling to Reader ministry in those who offer.
- They help *candidates* assess the extent to which their sense of calling matches what the Church is looking for in its Reader candidates.

This is, of course, precisely the same thing looked at from two sides, and is rooted in the idea of prayerfully discerning the will of God. Although we might think that the criteria have fulfilled their usefulness at the point at which someone is recommended for training for Reader ministry, the issues that the criteria raise continue to be relevant after the initial process of selection. The aspirations and expectations set out in the criteria can also provide a good checklist throughout training and beyond. As we have already noted, we are all 'works in progress' seeking to deepen our understanding, experience and maturity as people and as ministers (in so far as it makes sense to draw any distinction between the two).

In this chapter we revisit the criteria for Reader selection, not so much now to ask the question, 'Is this person called to this ministry?', but rather, 'How might the Church nurture the development of those selected for Reader training? What sort of minister does the Church expect and need him or her to grow into?' The criteria can help us focus here, and can be a useful tool for personal and ministerial development.

But first of all, let's look at one aspect of preparing for public ministry a little more closely. The process by which people develop into those to whom the Church can entrust its public ministry is sometimes called 'spiritual formation' or 'formation for ministry'. Each of these phrases takes us so far but they have their limitations, and they are more use as descriptions than narrow, confining definitions. We have to be careful with the words 'spiritual' and 'spirituality' as they are often used in a rather vague way to mean 'something a bit other-worldly'. The meaning of the word 'spirituality' as used here has to do with a person's own walk with God.

The word 'formation' has also had something of a bad press of late and seems to be used in all sorts of ways by all sorts of groups. It sounds as though it might imply something that is done to you by others – squeezing you into a box that doesn't take account of your individuality, or taking more account of the Church's need than of what people bring to their discipleship and ministry. The idea at the heart of 'formation' remains a good and relevant one and answers the questions:

- What sort of minister am I being formed into as I prepare to take on this ministry?
- Where is the balance to be found between my personal sense of calling and the needs and mission of the Church?
- What impact is this particular training for this specific ministry having on my relationship with God, my prayer life and the way in which I live out my discipleship?

The Christian gospel talks (if not in these exact words) about community, interdependence, mutuality and accountability. Ministry is not just an act; it isn't about acquiring a set body of knowledge or a particular set of skills to perform in front of others in an attempt to convince them to believe something. It is about expressing our passion for the gospel (and not just for the Church) and about letting the spark of God be seen in all that we are and do. The process of formation is about guarding and fanning that spark in order that we might become lights on the hilltop.

At the heart of all *form*ation, then, is con*form*ity to Jesus in whose ministry we share. So if it starts with *my* ministry, the benchmark must always be that it is Christ who calls us to share in *his* ministry. All Christians are called to be open to the power of the Holy Spirit at work in their lives, transforming us into the people whom God would have us be; this is something that all the baptized have in common. What is distinctive about formation for Reader ministry is that people are preparing to exercise a specific ministry within the life of the Church, a public, accredited ministry that has identifiable characteristics and parameters. Formation is a catch-all term for the impact that the mixed bag of opportunities for learning and development that comprises Reader training has on people, and it includes their own prayerful personal response before God to it all. Formation in this context, then, is about personal development, but not development in any direction. The Church needs people to fulfil particular roles and it pays for them to be trained to do so, but it remains, first and foremost, God's work in us, making us useful disciples and capable ministers.

We can see, then, how important it is that those training for (as those in) ministry seek to continue to:

- pray – not just in an ad hoc, 'on the hoof' way but in ways that will develop their relationship with God;
- work at discerning God's call on their life and at what this means in practice in the situations in which they find themselves;
- grow in their capacity to reflect theologically upon every aspect of life and faith and ministry;
- study scripture, and the other elements of traditional theology required for public ministry;
- work at putting 'classroom learning' into practical effect through the development of a range of practical skills for ministry.

As training progresses, the relationship between these different strands of training will gradually become clearer. 'Academic theology' will be seen to have a relevance far beyond essay writing as you begin to preach and teach and engage in whatever it is that the Church needs you to do. The skills you learn will find application in a wider variety of settings than you ever imagined when you started out. You will become more aware of links between your beliefs and the cries of a physically and spiritually hungry world. And long after you begin your Reader ministry you will, if you remain open to perceiving in your life that hand of God that has brought you to this point, continue to 'grow into' the role, continue to be conformed to Christ, and be effective in leading others to and in their life of faith.

Being part of a group or cohort of people training for ministry will help some of these less tangible, hard to define developments take place, and some aspects of the process of your being resourced or formed for ministry will happen almost without your realizing it: it will happen in the conversations that you have over a drink with your fellow students; in the casual encounters with people who ask why you are undertaking all this study; as you go about your daily life and business. But it will also need to happen in more consciously articulated ways, and this is why we revisit the selection criteria here.

There are lots of ways of handling the questions that follow; one approach won't suit everyone, and any single approach may not suit anyone all of the time. You may think that you know at a glance what will work for you personally, but try not to discount ideas that may not immediately seem attractive without first giving them a little thought.

Do you think best:

- when occupying your own space;
- when talking with a friend;
- in meeting with a more 'detached' person, such as a spiritual director;
- in sharing with a group?

Do you find it most helpful to:

- hold ideas in your head;
- write things down;
- draw pictures/illustrate/doodle?

Do you know what you think and then say it, or do you prefer to talk in order to know what you think? Do you have an instinctive feel for things, or do you prefer to spend time analysing carefully?

Bearing all of this in mind, here are some ways in which you might want to use the selection criteria and some questions based upon them (see below). Choose the one(s) that feel right to you.

1 Take time to sit quietly with the questions one by one, perhaps over quite a long period of time, maybe taking just one or two questions every now and then and prayerfully pondering their implications for your life/faith/ministry. Pray that God might enlarge your vision and help you to tease out what it means to minister in his name day by day, week by week, as you engage with the different elements of the training programme.

2 In your mind's eye imagine that Jesus is sitting in the room with you, talking to you about your hopes for ministry and about your training. Write down the conversation you have. You will need to listen really hard to do this, and you'll need to be brave enough to write what you actually hear Jesus saying rather than recording your own inner critical voice and attributing those thoughts to him.

3 Identify a small group of people with whom you can meet regularly (perhaps once per term) throughout your training. You might include your vicar, spouse, a friend, a church member or two. The group is best kept small – perhaps four people including yourself might be about the right size. Make sure that they are people whom you can trust to keep confidences and that you can be totally honest with them. Use the questions that follow as a starting point.

4 Find a spiritual director or other trusted individual with whom you can share anything that is important to you. There will probably be someone in your diocese who has the role of advising people here, or the person responsible for your training might be able to help you make contact with someone who is right for you. As part of your regular encounters talk openly and honestly about your training and the impact that this is having upon your walk with God, ensuring that, among other things, you cover the ground that the questions address.

5 Take a roll of paper – lining paper is ideal – and draw your responses to the different questions, perhaps sometimes jotting down notes, sometimes including pictures, diagrams or charts, whatever makes sense to you. Keep the same roll going throughout your training so that you can track changes and developments.

6 Keep a notebook or journal of your training and of the ways in which this relates to, interacts with and influences your ongoing, developing journey of faith.

You may already have developed your own way of achieving the same goal, but above all, don't do nothing! The quality of your learning and your ministry will be significantly enhanced if you spend time working at it, so consciously bring every aspect of yourself and your training before God. Rejoice in what is going well and hand over to him any fears, failures and limitations that might be holding you back and preventing your personal, spiritual and ministerial growth. As you do so, remember that while classroom-based learning is important and skills are necessary, much of the quality of what you will bring to ministry will be a reflection of your own journey of discipleship. Or to put it at its most simple: if you walk with God that will be evident to those around you; if you aim to equip yourself for ministry exclusively through your own effort, that will become evident too.

Consider these questions – not all at once, but bit by bit as your training unfolds. Some of them might take a little teasing out – but don't give up, it will be well worth the effort. As time goes on, try to be aware of changes in your responses. Don't be surprised or discouraged if some questions seem to become more difficult to answer, or even if you feel that you have 'gone backwards' rather than progressed. It's just as likely that you are engaging more fully with the deeper implications of the question.

We start each time with a summary of the relevant criterion.

1  Vocation: 'Candidates should be able to speak of their own sense of vocation to ministry and mission, referring both to personal conviction and to the extent to which others have confirmed it. Their sense of vocation should be obedient, realistic and informed.'

   (a) What is the relationship between your own personal sense of calling and the duty of the whole Church to set mission at the centre of its life?

   (b) How is your own way of relating to God being influenced by your call to ministry? Are you aware of any change or growth here?

   (c) How do you respond when you are facing a difficult situation in the Church or when you feel impatient with others?

   (d) What do you do when you fail or when you are frustrated with people or situations in the Church? Can you accept the inevitability and the reality of these and handle them constructively?

2  Ministry in the Church of England: 'Candidates must be baptized and confirmed and regular communicants of the Church of England, who are familiar with its traditions and practices.'

  (a) Try to identify the priorities and attitudes that exist within your own parish. Can you relate these to what they (and you) believe about God?

  (b) You are training to be part of the Church's public ministry. How do you understand the role of the Church of England nationally and your own church community locally?

  (c) In what ways, both in the past and now, have you been able to help people see the relevance of the Christian faith for their lives/culture/context? If in training for Reader ministry, has this changed since you were recommended for training?

  (d) Can you make links between the gospel and the world? Are you able to see and interpret the impact of social patterns and trends upon the work of the Church? Are there ways in which the Church might have an impact upon social patterns and trends?

3  Faith: 'Candidates should show an understanding of the Christian faith and a desire to deepen that understanding. They should demonstrate personal commitment to Christ and a capacity to communicate the gospel.'

  (a) Are you comfortable discussing issues of faith with others? Are you willing to allow your own beliefs and behaviour to be challenged? Are you confident (but not arrogant) about what you believe? Can you accept that others might differ from you without assuming that they must simply be wrong?

  (b) How do you handle doubt, in yourself and when expressed by others? What effect is your training having on what you believe?

  (c) Are you open to seeing God's presence and action in the whole of creation and in every aspect of life and experience?

  (d) Can you make connections between your own experience of life and the Christian tradition of faith? Can you reflect theologically upon your life and context?

  (e) Are you able to identify expressions of faith that are not consistent with your belief and that of the Church, either because they are false or because they are inadequate? How do you respond when someone firmly holds a view that is not consistent with Christian doctrine?

(f) Can you communicate your faith effectively and with conviction so that others might discern the purpose and presence of God in the world?

4 **Spirituality and worship:** 'Candidates should show evidence of commitment to a spiritual discipline which involves individual and corporate prayer and worship. Their spiritual practice should be such as to sustain and energize them in their daily lives.'

(a) Do you pray? Do you continue to pray when life is tough? What about when life is easy? Do you have a pattern of prayer that you aim to keep to? Do you manage this? How do you handle those times when it doesn't work out?

(b) Would you be confident in helping others to pray or in praying with others? If not, can you say why not?

(c) Are you developing an ability to preach clearly and honestly? Do you have the communication skills you need for ministry?

(d) Do you plan and prepare carefully when leading others in worship? Are you able to worship at the same time as leading others in worship? (Don't worry if you struggle with this initially – it will come with time.)

5 **Personality and character:** 'Candidates should be sufficiently mature and stable to show that they can sustain the demanding role of a minister and to face change and pressure in a flexible and balanced way. They should be seen to be people of integrity.'

(a) Think about your personal maturity, stability of personality and integrity of character. How do you assess yourself here? How do you think others see you? How do you know?

(b) How do you behave when God's will and your beliefs, feelings and desires don't coincide?

(c) Are you tempted to take yourself too seriously?

(d) Do you know both your strengths and your limitations? Can you admit it when you are wrong? Can you discuss mistakes openly with others where this is appropriate?

(e) Can you recognize the extent to which your own views are influenced by others – either by groups or individuals?

6 Relationships: 'Candidates should demonstrate self-awareness and self-acceptance as a basis for developing open and healthy personal and pastoral relationships as ministers.'
  (a) Do you establish and maintain a range of open and appropriate relationships?
  (b) Do you have the personal skills to relate effectively to people of varied age and personality, and of different social, ethnic and religious backgrounds?
  (c) Are you aware of and able to understand issues of sexuality, gender and power in relation to working with people of the opposite sex?
  (d) Have you developed the skills of working within appropriate boundaries of confidentiality? Can you show sensitivity when engaged in pastoral work with others?
  (e) Do you maintain appropriate boundaries between your public role and personal matters?

7 Potential for training: 'Candidates should be capable of undertaking satisfactorily a course of study and ministerial preparation with an open and enquiring mind.'
  (a) Are you able to integrate prayer, faith and theological learning, and value the part they will each play in the exercise of your ministry?
  (b) Can you engage with the ideas and thoughts of others, in print or in conversation, without either automatically taking on their thinking as your own, or refusing to be swayed by a better argument?
  (c) Can you set yourself goals to aim for, and work towards them with self-discipline and without being overly dependent upon constant support and encouragement from others?
  (d) Are you committed to lifelong learning?
  (e) Do you take seriously the need for appraisal, direction and guidance in your ministry?

8 Leadership and collaboration: 'Candidates should show the potential to offer wise leadership in the Church community and to some extent beyond it. They should also show ability and willingness to co-operate with other ministers and to work as team members as well as leaders.'

(a) Do you take seriously the challenge to all ministers to be servant leaders, providing an example of love and faith based on Christ's ministry?
(b) Are you aware of how your own strengths and weaknesses can have an impact upon other people (who have their own strengths and weaknesses)? Can you work as part of a team with different types of people?
(c) Are you becoming familiar with different styles of leadership and with developing your own ways of leading as they fit different types of situation?

Commitment, openness, reflection, integration: these words encapsulate much of what this chapter is about. But above all its purpose is to help you to make connections between every aspect of your training and your walk with God so that you might grow into an effective minister to the greater glory of God.

# 8

# After you have been licensed

We have looked at some of the core elements of initial training for Reader ministry; now we turn our attention to what happens after licensing. It is easy to imagine that once you have been trained and licensed as a Reader the story is now complete; the job is done. Of course, in reality, this is only the beginning of the story. Admission to the office of Reader marks the point on someone's journey at which the Church can say, 'We have confidence in this person, they can speak with a degree of authority on our behalf.' No matter how much someone has been involved in the life of their church, embarking on a public ministry in the Church is inevitably a time of transition. Ministry is service, but it is also a privilege; it is God's gift to us to be used in the Church on his behalf. In accepting this gift Readers acknowledge that the nature of their relationship with the Church as institution will change. Part of this change lies in the fact that ministry brings responsibility, and with responsibility comes added accountability. When Readers speak or act in the course of their ministry, they do so not just in their own individual capacity but on behalf of the Church.

Liz put it like this:

> Once I was licensed I became much more aware than when I was in training of being an 'official of the Church'. I'm still me, being myself, but I'm also a church representative and there are things that it isn't appropriate to say about the Church as a minister.

A further aspect of this changed relationship concerns the need to keep one's ministry both fresh and relevant. The best way of doing this, in addition to maintaining a healthy prayer life, is to engage in a broad range of opportunities for ongoing training.

## Developing the skills of theological reflection

Christians should never stop wanting to be disciples in the true sense of being 'pupils and learners'. There isn't ever a stage when we have been filled with a lifetime's supply of information, understanding and experience. Being a minister brings a special responsibility to be open to a constant refreshing and reshaping of our thinking and practice. It means being ready to meet a host of challenges and questions that bubble up in a changing society. It means being equipped to minister in tomorrow's Church and not yesterday's. This is where the skills of theological reflection that began to be learnt during initial training really begin to come into their own, as the new Reader considers the particular context and set of circumstances in which he or she ministers and asks, 'Just what does it means to occupy this space and carry out this role?'

- What does it mean to work in, for and on behalf of the Church in the place in which God has placed me?
- Just what *does* it mean to minister the gospel in a way that's relevant to those among whom I live and work?
- What does the Reader's blue scarf signify to people in our churches?
- What does it mean for me in practice to say that Reader ministry can be a bridge between Church and world, ordained and lay?
- How do I learn from the ministry in which I'm engaged today in order that I might become more effective tomorrow?
- How do I go about ensuring that I don't simply make the same mistakes over and over again?

The list of questions that we might pose is almost endless and some questions will have more relevance to some people in some situations than will others. If you remain alert to the need to ask questions such as these in a way that makes sense of your own particular context, you will develop your ability to reflect theologically as you gain experience both of the role and of your inhabiting of that role.

## Continuing with study

While the initial training period may be over, the work continues. Now more than ever there is a real recognition that all those in ministry – both lay and ordained – need to be offered by the Church good quality, worthwhile continuing ministerial education. In some dioceses this falls into two parts: (a) a programme specifically designed to meet the needs of those in their first few years of public ministry (often called Initial Ministerial Education (IME) 4–7 in recognition of the fact that the initial training period continues, though in a different way, beyond licensing); and (b) a more general programme open either to all in ministry or sometimes to all Readers separately. The name given to this varies from diocese to diocese.

By the time you reach the end of your course, it can be difficult to greet the prospect of more study with much enthusiasm. Surely now is the time to turn your back on the slog of study and put everything you have learned into practice? On one level, of course, this is true. Now is the time for you to begin to practise what you have learned. However, one of the things that you might have learned is that the best ministerial practice arises out of a thoughtful engagement between yourself, your context and theology. It is by drawing on the deep roots of scripture, church history, systematic theology, ethics and so on that your ministry can be most effective. As a rule, our contemporary society splashes in the shallows but yearns for something more. Many people express frustration with their lives and ask whether there is any more to life than 'just this'. Part of the ministerial task is, through preaching, teaching and pastoral work, to help people to explore a deeper and more profound relationship with God. In order to do this it is vital that you build up a stock of resources from your own reading, thinking and reflecting.

Some dioceses have good systems for drawing you into the task of thinking and reflecting on theology and ministry. Others are a little more stretched for resources and have less to offer. Whichever diocese you are in, it is valuable to take stock every six months or so and ask yourself what additional resources you might need to enhance your ministry.

Some questions you might like to ask are:

- Where have I felt at ease and confident in my ministry? Are there any resources (books, training days, courses) that I might use to enhance this part of my ministry?
- Where have I felt stretched and under-resourced in my ministry? Are there any resources (books, training days, courses) that I might use to enhance this part of my ministry?

You might also like to look in turn at specific aspects of your ministry – preaching, teaching and pastoral care – and undertake the discipline of reading a new book on one of those areas every six months (e.g. use a new commentary for your preaching, pick up a new book on liturgy, etc.) and ensure that you cover each area of your own ministry as a part of this.

## Ministerial Development Review

Another aspect of continuing your ministerial formation is Ministerial Development Review (MDR). This is now a national requirement for all clergy and an increasing number of dioceses now expect Readers to participate in it as well. MDR takes place at regular intervals (these vary from diocese to diocese but in practice would usually be every one to three years) and may be linked to the periodic renewal of the Reader's licence.

MDR can feel like a burden in an already pressured life, but it is very important indeed. It's when we are at our busiest that we most need to pause, stand back and reflect on what we're doing. Most dioceses have developed a form to help people with this task; it ensures that a wide range of areas of ministry and personal faith and spirituality are addressed in a way that affirms, challenges, nurtures and stretches each individual in ways appropriate to them. Whether or not you find filling in the form helpful, and whether or not the interview leads to clear action, undertaking an MDR is a good opportunity for a ministerial MOT. Some MDR processes are more developed than others. Whatever is offered in the place where you minister, even if it is excellent and beneficial it can also be good to take the time yourself to sit and reflect about your ministry and where it is going, and if this can be done with someone else, so much the better. Appendix 2 provides an example of an MDR form for Readers.

# Part 3

# BEING A READER TODAY

# 9

# Established expressions of Reader ministry in the Church

The ministry of God's people in God's world happens most effectively when the wider context in which people minister – the deanery, diocese and national Church – is confident in articulating that the engagement of Christian people in life, whether as disciples or ministers, is part of and set within God's overarching plan for the world. The way that Paul explains the impact of faith on people's lives is as relevant to us as it was to the first Christians. He doesn't write about faith in the form of long creed-like statements. Rather, he writes like this: 'Do not be conformed to this world, but be transformed by the renewing of your minds, so that you may discern what is the will of God' (Rom. 12.2). Being a Christian (and being a Church) does not mean withdrawing from the world, or keeping things to do with faith sealed off from the rest of life. Life in the 'real world' has to be a witness to the saving power of the cross and the transforming power and promise of resurrection. It means looking at life through a lens of faith that informs who we are, what our value systems are, and how we behave. It encourages us to see ourselves not as isolated individuals, but part of Christ's Body – which owes its existence to God's initiative of love towards the world, and not to human effort.

We cannot claim to be followers of Jesus when we are sharing in worship or fellowship with our brothers and sisters in Christ unless our being a Christian, whether as disciple or minister, radically affects who we are at the deepest level of our being. It's well recognized within the Church that most Readers strive hard not only in their overtly church-based activities, but in the (in many ways much more difficult) task of seeking constantly to find ways of integrating their faith and their ministry credibly into every part of their lives. It's the weaving of ministry into the weft and warp of everyday existence that gives it authenticity. It's the habit of reflective engagement in that ministry that ensures that the Reader is no mere church functionary but someone equipped and enabled to engage fully and confidently with the day-to-day life of our God-breathed, God-redeemed and God-sustained world. All of this is a way of saying that as ministers we need to remain alert to the grace of God that called us into ministry in the first place; it can be easy to develop habits that hinder rather than further God's purposes.

This considered and determined engagement in God's world is very evident in the stories that follow, stories that are as individual and unique as the people engaged in this significant ministry. They are stories of 'ordinary' people leading 'ordinary' lives whom God has called to share in the Church's ministry. We haven't gone out of our way to unearth startling examples of people who are doing dramatic things; we didn't need to. Perhaps the theology of Reader ministry – something over which the Church has tended to tie itself in knots in recent years – is to be seen most clearly not in theorizing about it but in celebrating its practical expression. For this reason we don't continue this chapter with a fully worked-out 'theology of Reader ministry' backed up by practical examples. Such a theology couldn't exist independently of actual Readers doing real ministry. Reader ministry isn't a concept or an idea or a theory but an outworking of God's gifts and graciousness in the lives of those who are called to it. Instead we offer here the words of a number of Readers and try to show just how much theological content there is in the day-to-day expression of this ministry as exercised by quite different people in very different contexts. All those whose words appear here are people who have responded, and who continue to respond, to God's invitation to them to commit in this particular way, in our own day and wherever they are to the furtherance of the Kingdom.

We'll begin with a number of people who are relatively new to Reader ministry, for whom the transition to this ministry is still very fresh, before hearing from others who have been involved for longer. They have all been honest enough not to put a 'holy gloss' on their ministry but to tell it how it is, for which we owe them a debt of gratitude. In each case the conversation opened with the question, 'What does it mean to you to be a public representative minister of the Church of England?', and it took its own course from there. What they had to say has been reproduced here almost exactly as they said it, so that the style and integrity of their stories might be preserved. We have inserted some numbers here and there so that particular ideas can be referred back to easily.

### Kate (Reader for one year)

For me discipleship is about placing Christ at the centre of life; it's about 'being in' Christ and being his hands and feet in the world in whatever way that happens to be. For me that's expressed through Reader ministry, for others it will be different. I know that I'm a representative of the Church as a whole, not just my local parish. There's a need for appropriate boundaries in ministry; you have to behave professionally but you have to be genuine too. I brought a sense of professionalism with me from my training as a counsellor, but this feels different – I know that I can let myself come through more. (1) In my Reader ministry I feel as though I'm being the person I'm meant to be. (2)

But it's not always straightforward embarking on a public ministry in the Church. A churchwarden in my parish couldn't accept my ministry when I began and I knew this early on; she saw some of what I do as a Reader as her ground. I was upset at first – though it wasn't really about me personally – and I felt frustrated. I guess she felt threatened and insecure and I had to be patient and try to understand where she was coming from. I'd been called into ministry and felt that I was being prevented from exercising parts of it. I've had to detach myself and let God be God in the situation. I could be more assertive but I've held back and tried to understand her. Thankfully, everyone else has been very positive and supportive. (3)

I see my role as trying to bring out the potential in people. There are lots of people who haven't identified their own gifts, and it's good – and very rewarding – to be able to help them to do so. I don't think, 'This is my job, keep off it'; I don't want us to become fixed and inflexible in our various roles, but permanently on the move, finding ways to support each other to be effective in our common witness. It's an ongoing process of allowing yourself to be moved by the Spirit. The frustration sometimes is that you're aware of this and it doesn't happen. I sometimes feel as though the Spirit is moving me in a particular way but that due to external factors that development is prevented from taking place – and when this happens I just have to wait.

As a minister it's all too easy to say 'Yes' all the time. We need to be conscious of balance. My ministry is rooted in prayer and without this I feel out of sync. You can get exhausted meeting the needs of others and then you can lose the capacity to be empathic. If you're not in a good place yourself you won't be much use to anyone else. You need to step back sometimes and identify your own needs, and balance your own home life and interests against meeting the needs of other people. But it's also about being a servant of Christ, so sometimes I have to lay my own stuff aside to be available for others. This can be the same for clergy, of course. You can become so preoccupied with the church and its needs that you end up acting as more of a business manager than a minister. For me, being energized comes through that time each day when I can be quiet with God, even though finding that time can sometimes be quite difficult. This is a side of my life that existed for many years before I embarked on Reader training – although being a Reader has helped to deepen it. I'm conscious that I must find those spaces and I know that if I don't I'm losing out, because my relationship with God is the crux of my ministry and of all that I do. (4)

There's a lot of respect for my role in the parish, perhaps because they're well used to Reader ministry, though my ministry is very different from the previous two Readers in the parish who were first licensed in the 1960s. They were much more formal than I am, but times have changed. (5)

### Liz (Reader for one year)

I've discovered that most people outside the Church have very little idea what a Reader is and when talking to people outside the church I usually refer to myself as a lay minister. I don't think they would see much distinction between a Reader and a curate, even though there's a big difference in my eyes. Since starting training I'd been aware that whenever I was speaking about the Church – which is not necessarily in church – I'm its representative. When I was licensed I became much more aware of being an 'official of the Church'. I'm still me, being myself, but I'm also a church representative and there are things that it isn't appropriate to say about the Church as a minister. I'd still express my views but would be more careful now about saying, 'These are my views and others hold different views.' Through my Reader training and ministry I've developed a broader understanding of how the Church works. I can sometimes listen to what people are saying and reply, 'Yes, but . . .', and bring in a different perspective, or I might be able to explain why things are as they are. Before, I would just have launched in. (6)

### Colin (Reader for one year)

Knowing I'm authorized and licensed gives me a degree of authority and confidence wherever I go. If I take a service somewhere new, people see me as someone with the Church's authorization and they're ready to listen to me. It makes me more able to go out and preach the good news of Jesus to people and to share my faith with them.

Having to prepare for leading worship means that I'm learning much more and spending more time with God – and being fired up. Lots of people say it's a pressure having to prepare sermons and services but I find the opposite; it energizes me.

I've often felt different from other Readers. When I began my Reader training course I found people were mostly from a different culture, from 'soft' occupations or retired people – generally people from what seemed to me to be a more relaxed way of life. (7)

During my training we listened to someone speak about her extensive funeral ministry; what she said and the way in which she said it just blew me away. She was truly humble but totally passionate and she really made her funeral ministry work. That form of ministry isn't for me but to hear someone talk in such a beautiful, quiet way made me want to do the things I'm good at with the same passion and degree of effectiveness. I found it really exciting.

Outside the Church it can be tough. The secular world really is getting the hang of being secular. Eighteen years or so ago when I became a Christian there was general goodwill towards the C of E and Christianity. Now I think it's seen as just another world-view to be discredited. The task inside the Church is to keep people's spirits high; outside the Church it's a much harder challenge. (8) Whereas people might once have given you the benefit of the doubt, now, in the media, government, our whole politically correct society, the drive to treat all religions equally often simply means that they all get pushed aside.

I'm a manager for an information technology outsourcing company, responsible for contract management, profit and loss, operational delivery – dealing with all aspects of IT on behalf of other companies, some of them global companies.

People know at work that I'm a Reader but they don't really mention it much. When I was licensed they were pleased and felt that I'd achieved something, but they shy away from religion. My faith and my ministry don't work against me because people have respect for me as an individual – but I've only been able to have three conversations that were overtly about God in the past two years. You can see people backing away all the time – they generally talk just about work and about little that's personal. In corporate terms, because it's a global corporation with people from lots of different backgrounds, great care is taken not to mention religion at all. My company doesn't have Christmas, it has festive celebrations – at £30 per head.

If people ask you how you are, the only answer they want to hear is that you're fine because that means that you're going to get things done. My working world is full of winners – 'We're the best, we can do our own thing and we don't need any help.' Someone was off work because they'd worked too hard, but they wouldn't hear the word 'stress' mentioned because that's a weakness. I pray for the company – Jeremiah said to pray for the prosperity of the place where you live and the place in which you work.

Abdul is a Muslim, but they see him as the guy who gets things done in a particular bit of the company. They don't see him as a Muslim and they don't see me as a Christian. They know I'm a Christian, they know I'm a Reader, but we both fit into their world by turning up and getting on with it. (9) I went through Lent without a drink once – at first I got lots of wind-ups but towards the end people were asking how I was getting on. People admire you when you do these things and stand up for your faith, but they don't want to be challenged by it. What impact do my faith and my ministry have on the company? My company like me being involved in ministry because I'm good at treating people equally, but that's probably about it.

## Philip (Reader for two years)

When I was licensed people started to ask more questions of me, and that led to me trying to understand more precisely what it was that I'd set out to do. I began to be regarded as a bridge-builder and a sounding board – and sometimes as a dart board too: 'Where's God now then . . . ?' Training made me feel more equipped to meet those expectations and to be able to respond to people with some degree of confidence. But I think that you're only going to be an effective bridge reaching out to people if the bridge is built in their direction. (10) There are a few very highly educated people who struggle with me being a Reader. I'll often write a sermon, then ask myself if a child, or someone at the start of their Christian journey (whatever their age), or some-one who isn't highly educated could understand it. I want to say things in a way that's appropriate to them. If I have to sacrifice how I come across to a few in order to reach the many I'll do it happily. Those who already know it all already know it all – those who don't, need a bit of clarity.

I own a hairdressing salon in my parish, so I work in the fashion industry. I'd wondered how my street cred would be affected when I became a Reader – a fashion adviser who'd found God. But that wasn't the case. God has always been there, but I've gained the confidence to share my faith. I sometimes see people who are more concerned with their nails than with paying off their credit cards. I often become aware of people's problems and sometimes have difficult decisions to make. It's hard when you read of a family's huge financial difficulties but are asked to provide them with expensive hair treatments. Occasionally I've lost clients because of the judgements I make. Some months ago a lady came to me who'd been to a different salon and had her hair permanently coloured – and all her family thought it looked terrible. She said that having it done in the first place and then attempting to sort it out had cost hundreds of pounds, but that she was still unhappy with the way it looked. I did what I thought best for her and it looked OK, but a few days later she phoned and said that she'd discovered that for £250 she could have had it put exactly right. I'd known that, but decided that as she'd already spent such a huge amount it wasn't appropriate to do it. I explained to her that I'd made a professional judgement, but she said that I was there to do exactly what she wanted, not to make professional judgements, and I haven't seen her since. Occasionally, too, I find myself making a decision that's pastorally right but that leads to the business suffering, such as when a key worker is facing a crisis and needs to be absent from work for some reason. (11)

I didn't make a big thing of it in my salon when I became a Reader, though people asked why I wouldn't be at work on a Saturday. When they found out, four of my 'Friday morning ladies' clubbed together and bought me my Reader scarf. One had written on the card, 'I hope it keeps you warm'. She'd kindly contributed but I don't think she really understood what it was all about. One of them goes to church and through conversations in the salon another has begun to attend too. Quite a few customers came to my licensing; some pretended that they were coming for the ride so they could do a bit of shopping, but they all came to the cathedral, too, to support me.

If someone opens up, you don't need to respond in a fussy way – but you have to listen and glean: are they conversing or opening their heart? For some years I've talked to someone whose family had been torn apart when one of them got into serious trouble with the police. It's not my place to gossip, but to listen and to choose my words carefully. I've learned not to respond too hastily; the conversation might start on a Wednesday afternoon in the salon and if it's someone from church I might say something by way of reply on the Sunday. (12)

I was approached once by someone who thanked me for something I'd done for the family eight months earlier. I had no idea that I'd reached this family in the way that I had. I'd prayed about the situation for months. People might be taken off the prayer board at church, but they still keep coming to mind. (13)

For me, engaging in ministry is about how best to serve; becoming a Reader was an opportunity to serve. I always want to combine my ministry with everyday life – and to do it as myself. In ministry we're meant to be ourselves, it would be wrong to try to be like someone else. (14)

Reader ministry is about being rooted in the community. (15) I hope that in a few years' time I might be able to be part-time in the salon and part-time working for the Church. I've always felt that becoming a Reader has given me an opportunity to serve. I'm excited by Fresh Expressions of Church and I'd love to be engaged in something like that. I know, though, that people are often keen to pour money into new ventures but less ready to support them subsequently. I'd like to be involved in something that supported people when the money – and perhaps people's energies – were in danger of running dry.

### Ian (Reader for five years)

I find public ministry to be a tremendous privilege. In my parish there's a certain respect for the office and a lot of support: the PCC pay for any training events that I undertake, for example, and this is written into my working agreement. At work they know I'm a Christian and I'll mention from time to time that I'm preaching on Sunday. The company I was working for when I was made a Reader profiled two people each month in their newsletter, so I arranged to be profiled just after I'd been admitted and licensed so that people would know. That company was in the same line as the one I now work for – one's a supplier to the other in the railway industry; we basically dig holes in the ground and fill them with concrete. I find that there's little opportunity at work to explore religious issues and increase people's under-standing. There are seven of us working in my office, including me and a colleague who's a practising Muslim. Whatever we are makes no difference to the company, which has no ethos that's relevant. It's recognized that I have a different set of values to many people, but I've never really been asked questions at work about faith issues. (16)

### Christine (Reader for ten years)

In church people can expect you to have all the answers as soon as you finish your training. I've worshipped in my parish since I was 19, more than 30 years ago, so they know who I am and where I'm coming from. Ministry separates you out a bit. People think I've got more authority than I have, even with regard to things they can do too, such as leading intercessions or administering Communion. People in my church won't administer Communion when there's a Reader present so I've had to devise plans to encourage them to be more involved. I don't want people to feel distanced from the life of the church just because I'm there as a Reader, and nor do I want to feel distanced from them. (17)

I'm just as much a public representative minister of the Church, of course, when I'm at work as a probation officer. A lot of what I do is judged on the basis of me being a Reader and in many ways this is positive. I do things that aren't necessarily my job but that I can just see need doing. They see me as a vicar-type-person who isn't a vicar. Recently I had a conversation with a colleague who's also a Christian, who said that she thinks people can change and that sex offenders ought to be given a second chance. I said that the evidence shows that people can't change their natural tendency and that the role of the probation service is more about helping sex offenders to manage their lives so that they can function in a way that's acceptable to society. She thought my perspective was unchristian, and I had to try to find a different way of saying it. There are lots of Christians at work but because they know I'm a Reader and have some author-ity given to me by the Church I'm the one people ask; they ask about what hymns they might choose for their wedding or they'll ask me to pray about something. People know that I won't gossip about what they tell me. But having said this, people don't really treat me differently – most of the time they get to know me first and discover that I'm a Reader as we begin to talk about what we do and what we're interested in.

My approach is fairly informal both at work and in the parish, but people have to know that there's some gravity there and that you'll deal with things in a professional way – but the profes-sionalism has to be tempered with who you are. I still need to be myself as a Reader because otherwise I'm rejecting my calling. (18) God called me as the person I am and he obviously thought that he could use me as that person. I haven't got to become someone else in order to minister. I'm myself as a probation officer – when I'm in court and put on a suit I'm still me. In the same way, I'm still myself when I'm in church and wear my robes.

## Les (Reader for twenty-five years)

Although I've been a Reader for a long time now I still find it a privilege to be entrusted with leading worship and preaching God's word. God has given me gifts in these areas and, through training and experience, has called me to use and develop those gifts. I value my ministry highly; even when it's hard work and pressured, or when I'm feeling tired I still see it as a privilege. I wouldn't say that this is something that I volunteered for as such – I felt compelled.

I've run a Christian bookshop for more than 30 years, so I can understand what customers want and I can help them to find the resources they need because I've done it myself; I've been preaching for over 25 years so I can help and guide them along the way. People often chat about a sermon or essay that they're working on; I know a lot of people and they know I'm a Reader. Clergy, Readers, other church people – especially those I've known for a while – talk about all sorts of things. They see me as a neutral person whom they can trust. They know I'll be on their wavelength. (19)

What are the challenges facing Reader ministry today? For many people I think it's the time needed to do the training, especially people with families or heavy work commitments. Sometimes people leave it until they retire – perhaps taking early retirement – so that they've got time to do it. I found it difficult all those years ago; even if people have the calling and the desire they've also got to have the wherewithal to do it. But as well as this, people don't always have the confidence – they need to catch the vision more and realize what's possible.

I welcome more lay people being involved; it's not only good but essential with the diminished number of clergy. I think people regularly involved in public ministry do need a good training but they also need to be encouraged. Personally I've never felt threatened by other people doing things and am pleased when they get involved. The harvest is great and we need more workers.

There are different ways of reading and reacting to these stories but there seem to be a number of key themes that have emerged.

## Being oneself in ministry

The stereotypical comedy minister (usually a vicar but the same thing applies) almost always talked in an odd, over-enunciated voice, was a figure of fun and wasn't presented as being a 'real person'. Furthermore there was often at least a grain of truth in the caricature. Kate, Philip and Christine (2, 14 and 18) make the same vitally important point, one that we discussed earlier, namely the importance of being oneself in ministry. It is the people we are, with all our gifts and faults, good intentions and failures, whom God, for reasons and purposes that we can sometimes find it difficult to fathom, calls into ministry. This isn't a mere superficial observation but contains a deep theological truth: we are acceptable to God because we have been made acceptable through the death and resurrection of Jesus. There is no other reason for us to respond than because we are called. This is vital to our understanding of all that we do in any capacity in Christ's name. This doesn't mean that as ministers we can be smug or self-satisfied; we are the clay in the potter's hand to be moulded as the potter wishes. It is only when we are truly ourselves – warts and all – that that shaping can take place. Our task is to minister in such a way that we don't attract attention to how clever or competent or effective we are – or for that matter how weak, humble and lowly. We are to shine in the world like the lights that Jesus talks about in Matthew 5.16–17.

## The parameters of ministry

Kate is alert to the differences between counselling and pastoral ministry as she has trained for both (1). Table 9.1 reminds us of some of the key differences. However, there are important lessons to be learnt from counselling and counsellors. It can be very easy for those in ministry to become caught up in pastoral situations that seem to be responding to genuine need, but that end up with the minister having to mark out boundaries when the person with whom they are working becomes overly dependent. The fact that this is most likely to happen with people who have a history of

**Table 9.1  Key differences between counselling and pastoral ministry**

| Counselling | Pastoral ministry |
|---|---|
| Formally structured with a set and limited time and place etc. | Often 'ad hoc', 'on the hoof' and in informal settings. |
| Agreed contract at the start of the relationship. | Contract not appropriate. |
| Often paid by the hour – 'professional'. | Time freely given – undertaken for love of Christ.* |
| Ongoing supervision a requirement. | May have 'spiritual director' or similar but in a more general capacity than supervision. |
| Relationship established solely on basis of counsellor's qualification and expertise. | Relationship based on authority invested in the minister by the Church, underpinned by shared faith. |

* This has always been the general principle of the Church. Even most of those who receive payment from the Church (mostly clergy but in rare exceptions Readers) are considered to receive a stipend rather than a wage. What this means is that those people are not thought of as 'selling' their time and expertise to the Church under the terms of a contract but instead they receive enough money so that they can live and give their time freely for love of Christ without needing to have another job as well.

feeling rejected – and who might therefore seek an inappropriate amount of attention from a pastoral encounter – can only serve to compound the situation. Furthermore, it can be seen not only as a rejection but a rejection by someone who is ministering in Christ's name. This illustrates the importance of the Reader being aware of the basic skills of the counsellor while at the same time being very clear that the ministerial role is a pastoral one. It is worth remembering the pattern of Jesus' own ministry, which is that he did not encourage people to cling to him in a dependent kind of way – rather, the opposite.

A Christian employer, especially one who runs a small business in the community in which they also minister, can face a real dilemma as Philip's story illustrates – motives and principles may be subject to more than usual public scrutiny (11). There may be times in running a business when the pastoral needs of an employee are in conflict with good business strategy, or when retaining an underproductive employee 'to be kind' threatens the jobs of many others. The simple, soft option is not always available.

Staying with Philip for a moment, one can easily see why people sometimes refer to a hairdressing salon as a modern-day confessional (12). Philip's faith and ministry inform the way in which he responds to people, and he is a skilled listener and can keep confidences. We can see from what Philip says that he is alert to where the boundary lies between what it's appropriate to say to someone in the context of his work and how he might respond in a ministerial capacity.

The same sorts of issues could arise for Les, the chief difference perhaps being that he works in an overtly Christian line of retail (19). People talk to him knowing that they can trust him, and that trust is the fruit of many years of taking the trouble to get to know his customer base.

## The expectations that people have

As Kate discovered, it can be difficult working with people's expectations (3). She expected to be free to minister only to find that she was being blocked at every turn. There are few things as disheartening as the sense that people are undermining or working against one's ministry. Earlier, we raised the need to be able to handle frustration and make use of it. Here is a good example of the patience that's sometimes needed in the face of a difficult situation that isn't of the Reader's making. Kate has not acted in a way that might have upset the churchwarden; it's simply her presence as a Reader in the parish that's being perceived as a threat to another church officer – a threat that wasn't evident until the day that she was licensed. She has chosen to stand back patiently, even though this has been a costly choice to make, and (as she puts it) 'let God be God' in the situation. She is aware that she could have taken a more assertive stance, and through her training as a counsellor, backed by her Reader training, has the skills to speak to the churchwarden about it in a non-threatening way. Kate is not the first person to enter ministry only to discover that others find their very presence threatening. How would you *ideally* hope to address this situation if you were in her shoes? How do you think you would *actually* respond?

Many areas of life have become less formal in recent decades, but in many situations there's a distinction to be drawn between being appropriately professional on the one hand – something that's required at all times, whatever the situation – and being formal/ informal on the other (5). Sometimes, as in the case of a funeral visit, a degree of formality and professionalism may go hand in hand. Especially with people you do not know, it's important at the outset to signal that you respect them by the way you speak, act and dress. But it's important to combine respect with warmness and care, and not confuse formality with coldness. At other times one can be equally professional while adopting a much more informal stance. Do you rejoice in or bemoan the increasing informality in society and in the Church?

Alongside this is a question about separateness in ministry (17). Christine says, 'I don't want people to feel distanced from the life of the church just because I'm there as a Reader, and nor do I want to feel distanced from them.' Readers will respond to this in different ways: some will want to lay down clear boundaries and relate to people only in a 'professional' manner; others will consider that this is not appropriate for ministry and will seek to avoid any kind of distance.

- Do you think that some degree of distance in Christian ministry is desirable or undesirable, to be encouraged/accepted or to be discouraged?
- Would you give the same answer with regard to the clergy? If you would answer differently can you say why?
- What are the advantages and disadvantages of maintaining a distance?
- What are the advantages and disadvantages of establishing no distance?

In reality you will probably do a bit of both, but thinking it through will help you to come to the decision that best fits you and your context. It is also worth talking it through with others in your ministry team. If others keep a distance and you do not you could risk undermining their ministry.

## Ministry is underpinned by prayer

Kate articulates clearly her dependence upon God for all that she is and does (4). Perhaps it should go without saying – but it's nonetheless worth stating here – that all ministry needs to build upon a solid foundation of prayer. In this regard ministry simply extends that central plank of all discipleship – the expression of a prayerful relationship with God in Christ through the power of the Spirit that informs all that we are and all that we do in Christ's name. You might think that this is stating the obvious but most of us need to be reminded more often than we need to be instructed, so it stands here as a reminder of one of the central tenets of our faith. If we try to 'go it alone', whether out of laziness, complacency, arrogance, forgetfulness or despair, our discipleship will come unstuck, and with it our ministry.

Philip's assertion that the need to pray for particular people and situations often continues long after they have been taken off a church prayer list is an important one (13). Very often the most pressing issues are those in the news headlines or the acute needs of those around us. But there are many chronic needs too, both with regard to the world at large and in relation to the people around us, that are still there day after day, week after week. Philip's words stand as a reminder that our prayers are not simply to be a God-directed rerun of the day's news headlines!

## Being loyal

What Liz says reflects the view that ministry, as well as bringing with it responsibility and accountability, also demands loyalty (6). This holds her back from expressing a view or opinion about the Church too readily. Do you agree? This raises a number of questions which again are worth reflecting upon:

- To whom is the Reader required to be loyal? To the incumbent? To the bishops and archdeacons of the diocese? To the views or motions of the diocesan synod? To the views expressed by the House of Bishops or the legislation passed by the General Synod? To 'the Church of England' as by law established?
- How can loyalty be balanced with expressing views with which others might not agree?
- Would you be happy expressing views about the Church within the Church but not outside it, or do you consider this to be a false distinction?

- How do loyalty and the call to speak prophetically, disturbing the comfortable, fit together?
- Can you think of any areas where you might, in the future, find your loyalty tested?

Again, it is worth thinking about this now. There will almost certainly come a time in your ministry when you will need to make this difficult decision – deciding what you think before the occasion arises can be helpful.

## The interface between church and secular cultures

This distinction between Readers in 'soft' occupations that are concerned with caring, nurturing, serving, guiding others and 'hard' occupations ('My company digs holes on the railway and fills them with concrete.' 'We are a company that expects its staff to be winners.') is an interesting one (7). Do we really equip people as a Church to engage with the tough realities of much of the contemporary world of work, where (for example) aggressive and successful competition is often seen as a virtue? Does our preaching help those followers of Christ whose daily lives are lived in such contexts to engage with them meaningfully? Or do we too often perhaps treat church as something of a refuge from the tough stuff and leave people short-changed and with the concerns of their workplace unaddressed? Is it perhaps that tough working environments don't encourage people to engage in family chat and the exchange of personal information, or is it to do with success – working in a company of 'winners' doesn't encourage people to reveal their vulnerabilities. Or perhaps again it's a straight gender divide, though from this (admittedly tiny) sample it would seem not. Does it make sense to talk about a divide between soft and hard occupations? Or does everyone have an element of both in their work?

We can no doubt empathize with Colin, but do you agree with him when he says, 'The task inside the Church is to keep people's spirits high; outside the Church it's a much harder challenge' (8)? Does this approach feed Christians in order that they may be sustained for their engagement with the secular world or might it create the dichotomy between two parts of life which we said earlier was a false one?

This raises an interesting question – my own initial internal response was 'Good, they don't see Abdul as a Muslim – that shows that he's integrated and accepted', but then, 'Oh – they don't see Colin as a Christian, that's not so good' (9). There's clearly something of a paradox here. What might be an appropriate response?

## Reader ministry as a bridge ministry

This is a metaphor that has caught the imagination in recent years; Readers can be seen as bridges between secular and sacred, clergy and lay, the 'temple' and the marketplace (10). Philip points out that a bridge is only useful if it reaches out in the right direction. The Archbishop of York, John Sentamu, preaching at a service at which he admitted and licensed 12 new Readers in November 2008, said that while the idea of a bridge can be a helpful one it can some-times feel as though the bridge is reaching towards a boat that is forever moving on the water. Just when you think you know where it is and reach out to it, it's moved off somewhere different. So the bridge image has its uses but is perhaps rather too static to encap-sulate the sort of dynamic, flexible ministry that Reader ministry needs to be.

Another problem is that the image of a bridge assumes that the Reader 'bridges' two entirely incompatible worlds – the church and world or the clergy and laity. Neither of these ought to see them-selves as 'opposites'; perhaps the role of a Reader might be to find ways of showing people how these categories are not opposed after all.

Working 'in the community' reflects Jesus' engagement with the 'marketplace' (15). He didn't restrict himself to mixing with people in the synagogue (though he worshipped and sometimes taught there), nor did he just spend time with the overtly religious (though he spoke with them and issued them challenges). Do you think that the Church – and Reader ministry in particular – is sufficiently 'in the marketplace' in our own day? Do you see Fresh Expressions of Church as helping to make this connection or is the Fresh Expressions task a different one?

# 10

# Diverse expressions of Reader ministry in the Church

We have reflected upon the stories of a number of Readers and have considered some of the issues and challenges that their ministry raises. Some Readers, as they gain more experience of ministry, find that following God's leading takes them into other specific ministerial contexts, often beyond the parish and their daily lives of work and home. We will hear now from a number of Readers who have taken such a step. This time we haven't provided questions to prompt your theological reflection, though perhaps you might like to spend a little time teasing out some of the underlying theological issues raised by each of these contexts.

For Jackie, Alison and Peter, whose stories we will read in a moment, this development of their ministry took them into chaplaincy. Colin holds a post as a Mission to Seafarers chaplain that had previously been held by clergy. A condition of his employment was that he trained as a Reader in order that he might engage with the theology, skills and formation expected of someone who was to hold the Church's licence to minister. One of the characteristics of chaplaincy is that there is a degree of commonality between all its expressions, while at the same time every context is highly distinctive – even those that on the face of things look similar because they are worked out within the same kinds of institution. Other Readers (such as Jenny) contribute to the work of chaplaincies without themselves becoming formal chaplains. Sylvia remained in parish ministry but, in a mould-breaking way, becoming a (half-time) stipendiary Reader with responsibility for a four-church benefice.

Jenny goes into a prison as a volunteer every Monday. She draws attention to some of the difficulties of this type of ministry:

We run Alpha in the prison about three times per year. We can't have any food – both because of the risk of drug smuggling and because they are not allowed treats. You never know who you've got there. People can be transferred to the other end of the country between sessions of a course that you're running. Relationships are built up quickly and then people disappear. You can't assume that anyone can read so you wouldn't ask someone to read a Bible passage. People will talk quite freely and trust will build up – though it's always difficult to know how much they're saying things simply to comply. They get an easy chair and people to talk to. The chaplains know that I'm a Reader but there are other volunteers in the chaplaincy too.

Jackie Farline was a chaplain to HMP Hull for 12 years.

My first time in prison was scary – I went in to play the organ for the Sunday service. That was all I did and gradually I got used to going in.

Then I began training to be a Reader within my church, and the prison chaplain said, 'We'll have to get you to do something more than just play.' I wasn't sure! A little while later I met a prison chaplain's wife on a training weekend who said, 'It draws you in, you'll end up doing more.' I thought not!

Some months passed, then one of the female lay chaplains at the prison left and I was asked to take her place. After praying, I felt that God was saying 'Yes'. So in obedience – not to mention fear and trembling – I went! The chaplain gave me a guided tour and then explained what I would be expected to do. With everything he mentioned, a light went on in my head – I've done something like that before, I thought. It was as if God had been preparing me for this ministry for many years without my knowledge.

I stayed for 12½ years and can honestly say that it was the most rewarding time I have ever had. It was a challenging time also, but I learnt so much from those around me.

Many of the prisoners had never given God a thought before but now they had lots of time to think and it was a joy to chat to them about Jesus and all that he had done for everyone. Some would challenge me: 'God breaks his own commandments so why should we follow them?' was one of them. I prayed much for wisdom and often had to admit that I didn't know all the answers!

As a prison chaplain I could do everything that was needed. Most people there didn't know or understand about Holy Communion, so most of our worship was non-eucharistic, and as a Reader this was very freeing; I was just one of the chaplains and was able and expected to do whatever cropped up on my duty days. It was also a joy to share in the work with those of other denominations – we were all there to serve God and any differences we had were of secondary importance. Again, most of those we worked with didn't understand them anyway. Our task was to preach a simple gospel message and point people to Jesus.

Something I read at the start of my time in the prison came to embody a lot of what we did as chaplains: 'People don't care what you know, until they know that you care.' It was so true – when we met up with prisoners, they weren't interested if we went in preaching. But if we took time to listen to them and their concerns and problems, then gradually a lot of them would ask why we did it and then we could explain about the God who loved them and who had sent his Son to die for them – and they then listened to us, because we had taken the time to show that we cared first.

The Sunday services 'inside' were very different from the ones I took outside. We had a captive audience, and although we knew that many came just to get an hour out of their cells, some would come because they wanted to worship God, and they would tell others off if they tried to disrupt things. One thing I found was that if during the prayers I asked for silence so that each one could bring their own concerns before God, you could have heard a pin drop; more so than in a lot of churches I have been in!

There were many statutory duties for chaplains to complete each day, as well as meetings to attend and admin to keep on top of, but I certainly felt that the most important task we had was to get alongside those who were most in need and give them the time they required – doing it all in prayer and trusting that God would bless what we did and bring fruit from it. There were some converts – only a few, but we could never know what happened to anyone after they left us; we had shared the gospel with them and the rest was up to God.

Alison Fisher, now an ordained hospital chaplain, began her hospital ministry as a Reader.

I was a Reader for many years until the Lord in his wisdom and humour called me to the ordained ministry. As both Reader and priest I had the privilege and joy to be a hospital chaplain within a mixed team of ordained and lay ministers. When I joined the team it was a natural progression of my ministry with the sick, dying and bereaved, which was very much part of my work in the parish. I appreciate that this is not a ministry that all Readers will feel called to and I was fortunate that I felt comfortable in hospitals having worked in them previously, and having been a patient on numerous occasions.

As a lay chaplain, I worked with the whole spectrum of patients, but particularly with the elderly, who were often without visitors, and with the newly bereaved parents of babies and young children.

I worked in a team in which each chaplain was allocated certain wards, so we got to know the staff and the ward routines. By working sensitively I found that I was happily accepted by patients and staff as a member of the chaplaincy team even though I didn't have the 'badge' of a clerical collar. Most patients are just happy to have someone who has the time to sit and listen to them; some like to have a prayer said with them and some like to receive Holy Communion or anointing for healing and peace. All of these can be led by a Reader; it's an opportunity to serve people at a time when they're feeling their most vulnerable. Readers can also sit and pray with the dying and comfort the bereaved, and may be asked to assist with worship in the hospital chapel. As a valued voluntary chaplain, the Reader can usually fix his or her own regular times to visit within the limits of the ward routines.

All people have a spiritual dimension to their being, even though this may not be expressed in a religious way, and most people on coming into hospital suddenly feel stripped of their independence and have time to think about what their life is about. To have someone who can listen to them sensitively, and share in their vulnerability and concerns, is a gift which most people greatly appreciate. It's a ministry that requires a patient listener who is sensitive and perceptive, happy just to sit in silence and hold someone's hand – and someone with a good sense of humour who doesn't take themselves too seriously.

Peter Blakemore is a Reader in the Diocese of Sheffield and Chaplain to South Yorkshire Fire and Rescue Service.

I began my Reader ministry in the Diocese of Sheffield in 1991, working with my parish for some years doing the usual things, leading services, preaching, etc. I still enjoy doing all of that, but it became obvious to me in other contexts – as a Scout leader and in my work for the Blood Transfusion Service – that I was often the only Christian minister, lay or ordained (or even the only 'out of the closet' Christian) whom people came into contact with. I realized that if I was not an ambassador of Jesus' word there would be many people who could say, 'I have not heard the message.' I'd often heard the call, 'Who will go and who will tell them?', but I thought it was meant for someone else. It took a long time for the thought to penetrate that if I kept on looking for the right person with the right words and lifestyle and time to do the job I could be looking for ever, so perhaps God would put up with me doing it until he found the perfect candidate for the job.

At times I felt rather caged in the Church and I wanted to be out in the wide world. I'm not brave enough to stand in shopping centres delivering the gospel, so I worked on being a strong, reliable witness to Christ in scouting and at work. This is often difficult and dangerous; people talk differently to you when you stand up for things you believe in. Being faithful to the people we minister to outside the Church can mean that we sometimes have to miss services or meetings inside the Church, and some people find this difficult; but we are often the only servant of God whom people see, and we have to be all that a good servant should be.

Some years after I had become a Reader I heard about the Industrial Mission in South Yorkshire. Interested, I contacted them and when I heard about the work they were doing I knew that this was the sort of thing I had been seeking to be involved with. They found me a position as a chaplain. This rather floored me as I was 'only a Reader' and felt that surely they would need at least a 'qualified vicar' for this type of ministry. However, God made it clear that this was where he thought I should be. There are chaplains for all sorts of organizations: steel works, retail stores, the police and the fire brigade. I was appointed to the Fire and Rescue Service. IMSY is interdenominational but all the chaplains must come under the authority of a particular Church. We work together as ministers of God's one Church, ministering the good news of the gospel to people at work.

I look after two stations in Sheffield, one on a large estate and a more out-in-the-sticks station which looks after large stretches of motorway and notoriously dangerous urban roads. Although it took a while to get to know some of the firefighters I now feel quite at home there. I've also been trained in counselling skills and I go as a representative of the Church to listen when they want to talk, to talk when they want to listen and to be a target at times – and to join in the banter. It's the sort of place where you can just drop in for breakfast – if you dare. I once said that I'd just have a couple of slices of toast and was presented with a whole loaf cut sideways into 'a couple of slices'. We all have many tales to tell! I was on duty as a chaplain at the world firefighter games when news came through that a firefighter had fallen off a ladder and was en route to hospital. I was dispatched to meet him on his arrival. As he arrived, he woke up and, on seeing my official chaplain's T-shirt, sat up, declared that he was not about to die and almost leapt off the stretcher.

We are sometimes asked to bless fire engines – rather like the launch of a ship – and to speak at commendations when brave acts are rewarded with certificates from the Chief Fire Officer. As chaplains we stand beside the firefighters as they serve the community; we drink tea, chat, generally 'look after' them, and pray for them all.

So where is God in all this and how does it relate to our calling? When Joseph and Mary journeyed to Bethlehem they didn't go to the synagogue or to the Pharisees' houses, they headed for the pub where normal people went, and when they found no room they agreed to stay in the shed. Throughout the Bible Jesus was found among the workmen and not often in the religious places. Of course, he was also at ease among, and able to communicate with, the learned teachers, and we hear on more than one occasion that he spoke with authority. But Jesus also grew up working with his hands in his dad's joinery workshop, and much of his ministry was spent among the fishermen. This to me is a call to get out of the Church and take the message to people who wouldn't ever know that the Church even cares.

Colin Worswick is Port Chaplain at Tees Port.

I have worked for the past seven years as the chaplain at Tees Port in Middlesbrough, one of the busiest ports in Britain. I'm also linked to a local church where I occasionally lead worship and preach. Outside of my chaplaincy and Reader work I also exercise a pastoral role in bereavement care and counselling, and in prison visiting.

Within the port there is a clearly designated pastoral role. My ministry is one of service, working with those who would be considered, on a world scale, to be among the poor and exploited. There is also a significant prophetic role in the promoting of justice and solidarity with a marginalized, mostly 'Third World' and Eastern European, workforce.

Certain key areas of my ministry have been directly informed by my core Reader training, including collaborative working, spiritual refreshment and development, and gospel interpretation and application – both in my preaching and in the analysis of my daily work experiences.

On a more personal level, in my final year of Reader training, I learnt the most valuable lesson of all when I began to appreciate that there can be genuine differences in styles of worship and biblical understanding but that these differences need not destroy unity within the wider Christian fellowship; on the contrary, they can enrich and contribute to it. I also discovered in tutorial sessions during training that it was possible to think theologically 'outside the box', but that any arguments that I presented needed to be based upon solid thinking and I needed to have a proper rationale to back up my ideas.

During the course of my ministry I have come to value the importance of working collaboratively. Good collaborative working is dependent upon respect and interaction. Characteristic of the levels of collaboration on Tees Port is the shared ministry, shared purpose and objectives, and shared decision-making that exists between the Anglican Mission to Seafarers, the Roman

Catholic Apostleship of the Sea, the German Seafarers' Mission, and on a wider scale, the local Hindu Cultural centre.

At the heart of my work on the port are many opportunities to identify and share in the often frustrating and difficult issues that face workers in the maritime industry. These include long distance relationships, absence from partners and children, fears of illness, and despondency. Seafarers often face humiliation and bullying at work, long hours, low pay, unsafe working conditions and poor accommodation.

I have met such kindness from strangers who visit our shores. Welcomed aboard their ships, I am offered food and warm hospitality from people who often have very little for themselves. When I meet them again during the evening in the seaman's club they share the stories of their lives and honour me with their confidences and their friendship. These small, often impoverished, transient communities have much to teach about fellowship and support and acceptance of people in a society where race, colour and creed don't matter.

The apostle Andrew did not attempt to give his brother Peter merely a description of the one who could well prove to be the way; he said, 'Come and see.' I attempt, through our Port tours, to follow his lead. The dynamic development of a ministry to seafarers in a rapidly changing world industry calls for constant analysis and understanding. But the first and most immediate imperative is that the seafarers should be met where they are. Both of these are the task of the Port Chaplain.

Sylvia Rice-Oxley was a half-time stipendiary Reader with responsibility for an East Yorkshire benefice of four churches from 1999 to 2008; she has recently been ordained. Some Readers are 'in charge' of a particular church within a benefice, working under the direction of the incumbent. The legal complexities to which Sylvia refers were the consequence of the benefice being vacant.

I was admitted as a Reader about 14 years ago and worked in the parish where my husband was incumbent. I had found the study so interesting that I went on to complete a degree in theology and ministry. When we moved to a different diocese the suffragan bishop invited me to take on a group of small parishes

that had been vacant for two or three years. It had been adver-
tised as a part-time post and putting me in as Reader in charge
was something of a last-ditch attempt at finding someone. It
took quite some months to set it up as there were both legal and
practical difficulties to be negotiated; in fact, nothing had been
finalized when the bishop moved to a new post six months later.
Letters passed to and fro and there was a lot of discussion about
who was actually in charge of the parish. I received a letter from
the Registrar to say that having a Reader in charge simply couldn't
be done under English law, but one way or another we made it
happen. It was decided that I should be in charge in the practical
sense of being responsible for ensuring that all the services were
covered and that sort of thing, and I was paid a part-time salary.
There was a titular priest in charge who signed faculties etc. as I
had no legal right to do so. A visiting bishop inducted the vicar
as priest in charge, then looked at me and said, 'I don't think we
need to go through all of that again, we all know that you're
going to be doing the work.' And that was that. All of this raised
a lot of questions in people's minds. The nominal priest in
charge's licence made it clear that he had the 'cure of souls' and
yet the general message was that the Reader in charge would be
doing the job of incumbent. My licence referred to me as Reader-
in-charge, but then stated that I was to exercise the office of
Reader 'under the general direction' of the priest-in-charge,
though there was never any expectation that he would be called
upon to do anything but perform the legal functions that I could
not undertake myself as a lay person. It is important for me to
state that I am not saying this to be critical of anyone – all
involved were committed to making things work out in the best
possible way. The chief difficulty lay with the legal framework
within which we were operating, as this made certain assump-
tions about benefices and incumbents and Readers that our
experiment simply didn't fit.

Looking back now I realize that I was thrown in at the deep
end. We pulled together, the parishes and I, and we made it work.
It's been a wonderful job; the churchwardens and PCCs and I
have worked as a team and we've undertaken major works on
the four church buildings. Financially, with four ancient buildings, four sets of insurance, four lots of bills, etc., it's very difficult

to pay the parish share. There's just one school between the four villages and I do a lot there – I'm also a governor. There are only 2,000 people in the benefice, of whom about 35 to 40 attend each week, though for special services we get up to 120 – and a bereavement service clearly met a need as we had a congregation of about 50.

I covered all the aspects of the work that I could as a Reader, including lots of funerals, at a time when Readers didn't really take that many. I did the usual round of ministry in a rural bene-fice; four harvests, four carol services and so on. My husband was a vicar and I often used to pop into my husband's study and ask, 'What would you do here?' When my husband retired he said he hadn't realized just how much I did! Looking back I feel that I wasn't really trained for all that I did and I learnt a lot of it 'on the job'.

I had always stood up for lay ministry, but first the suffragan bishop and then the diocesan said that they thought I ought to be ordained. It was suggested to me that a sense of call can come via the Church. I was ordained deacon in 2008. I feel I've grown into this role. People say, 'You're the same but different', or, 'You have authority now.' I think I've become more confident now and that reflects a big change in my thinking. I expect that deacon to priest will seem a bigger difference than Reader to deacon. Once I was ordained deacon I felt a difference. I don't feel that I'm better than anyone else at all but it's to do with the role and how people perceive you.

If someone else were offered this sort of role I'd say, ensure that there's sufficient support in place, a monthly review, a men-tor, etc., and a more active priest-in-charge whom you could go to and discuss things with. The bishop assured the priest-in-charge that he'd have no more work to do if he took this group on in a nominal sense; cover was provided by a number of other people. Lots of things developed over the years and with the benefit of hindsight I think that some of it could have been put in place earlier. We were working it all out as we went along.

But having said that, my being given the opportunity to be in charge of a benefice as a Reader (in reality if not legally) was a brave experiment, and I do believe that the Church needs to experiment. The legalities were immensely complex; perhaps

Canon Law sometimes needs to catch up with what's happening on the ground. I would like to see more experiments of various kinds take place that involve Readers in taking responsibility for parishes.

All of these examples are drawn from the experience of actual Readers. By including them we are simply describing some aspects of the current complexity that exists within the Church with regard to its ministry. We have deliberately provided no commentary here in the expectation that these stories will raise a whole host of questions and issues upon which you can ponder for yourself. The variety that you will find here demonstrates the breadth of practice with regard to Reader ministry in today's Church. Some people will feel that this practice is too broad, others that it is not broad enough. It is not our intention here to adjudicate, but simply to describe the experiences of Readers in many different ministries and by doing so to invite you into the interesting, yet complex, debate about the implications of current practice.

# 11

# Fresh Expressions of church and Reader ministry

## Setting the scene

'It is a function of human vanity to regard one's own age as an age of crisis.' These words of David Bagchi, a Reader in York diocese, speak into our present situation. People so often like to imagine that things are worse now than they used to be: 'Young people today are all hoodied hoodlums'; 'Fifty years ago every church was full on a Sunday'; 'You used to be able to leave your door unlocked and no one would ever think of burgling your property'. Well – perhaps, or perhaps not!

This word 'crisis' is one that we hear with increasing frequency within the life of the Church. 'The Church is in crisis; its finances are in crisis; its confidence is in crisis; its ordained ministry is in crisis; Reader ministry is in crisis . . .' It can be difficult to work out exactly what this means, and of course the word 'crisis' won't mean the same thing each time it's uttered. Underlying this are some big core themes: there are fewer clergy (and most conspicuously, fewer stipendiary clergy) than there used to be; Reader numbers on the other hand have experienced a steady increase in recent decades (though the numbers applying for training have recently dipped a little), but the average age of those being admitted is fairly high; money is short and costs are rising; society has changed and there are different views in the Church as to how much it should embrace these trends and to what extent it needs to stand apart from them.

Without doubt the average age of many congregations is increasing. Almost 20 years ago a priest was heard to say, 'I'm not too concerned that the Church is full of old people; I've always ministered to old people and they have simply been replaced by more old people.' We could no doubt critique this from a number of perspectives, but the two most important observations to make in this context are, first, the good news of Jesus Christ is for all people, whatever their age and circumstance. If we are not reaching out to all we're not as fully engaged as we might be with the world to which Jesus came and for which he died. Mission is one of the central planks in God's purpose for the Church; we are charged with the responsibility of trying to reach all. Second, from a purely practical point of view, if, as is the case, there are fewer younger people who know even the basic stories of Christianity, there will soon be few older people who know them. Former generations might have drifted in and out of the Church, perhaps returning to it in their retirement years, but we are now firmly in an age when that basic level of engagement and understanding is no longer present; very many people have no meaningful experience of church in their lives to which they might return.

Fresh Expressions of church is not simply about finding ways of stemming the decline in traditional congregations. In common with most of the Church in the West, the Church of England has seen changing patterns of belonging and attendance during the past century or so. This shift, which is still taking place, is having a significant impact upon the Church's ministry, including Reader ministry. It's not that the picture was entirely static before then, but there was a general assumption in society that most people who did not belong to another Christian tradition (or who weren't adherents of another faith) broadly regarded themselves as 'C of E'. For many this was expressed through weekly or near-weekly church attendance. Others would go to church regularly but infrequently, say at Christmas, Easter and Harvest; they were quite clear that it was the Church of England that was the church they chose not to attend very often. Nowadays the pattern is very different:

- Sunday mornings have to compete with a wide range of other activities, especially for families, who often find that church clashes with children's sport and other commitments.
- There is the (perhaps not altogether unreasonable) expectation that if people are to attend anything at all it should be of high quality, personally relevant and, if not actually entertaining, then at the very least engaging and dynamic – which for many people means that it should include images, and not consist of spoken or written words alone.

- The average age of congregations is often very high, with whole generations missing in many places.

Of course churchgoing reflects what is happening on a wider front:

- People are more autonomous than they once were; they feel less obliged to conform to the social patterns of a generation or two ago and more confident about expressing their individuality. 'I do church, he does golf, she works and they find that Sunday morning is the best time of the week for some "quality family time".'
- There is generally less regard for the authority of institutions of any kind, government, church, monarchy, etc., than there was in the past.
- The idea that the Church might have not only a right but also a duty to speak into society is challenged frequently by those who have no time for faith or for religion, or who feel that church is either a deeply personal affair, or a nice little sideline for people who can't find a more worthwhile focus for their energies. As one recent commentator put it, many see religious belief as a 'private eccentricity'.
- Those in public life who have a Christian faith that guides their daily living are often advised not to talk about it for fear that people will take them less seriously.

The reasons for the changes in society and Church are myriad but the outcome is clear: the setting for primary mission, instead of being a far-off country, is here, on our doorsteps and in our neighbourhoods. How might the Church respond? The initial response came not from 'the Church of England' centrally but from individuals who, prompted by the Holy Spirit, set about interpreting the gospel in new ways that would address the needs of today. In other words, the Fresh Expressions initiative did not begin as a strategy put in place by the Church but was the result of local people identifying local opportunities for engagement, and experimenting with ways of addressing people's changed life patterns and concerns. The intention is not, of course, to abandon gospel values in favour of a different message, it is simply to find a new voice in which the unchanging message of God's graciousness towards us might be heard: Jesus is not simply a good man from the pages of history who met an unlucky and unfortunate death; he is alive now, speaking to you in your situation, whoever you are and whatever your life is like. Ministry has never been static: every age has sought its own ways of drawing people into a living relationship with the living God. To take just one example: the ways in which the Revd Geoffrey Studdert Kennedy (Woodbine Willie) exercised his ministry on the Western Front during the First World War was both new and radical, but it probably wouldn't be accurate to call this a 'fresh expression' of church. The term 'Fresh Expression' really only makes sense within the context of today's post-Christian society, in which an understanding and acceptance of the values of Christianity among the majority of people can no longer be assumed.

New ways of being church have rarely begun in dramatic ways; they are, more often than not, the result of one or two people praying through a situation until it becomes clear what God is asking them to do, and then taking the risk that their idea might fail and trusting God to guide them.

## Being mission-shaped – looking beyond the traditional parameters of church

As more and more local developments appeared, the national Church committed itself to supporting and encouraging such experiments. In 2004 the Church of England set up its Fresh Expressions initiative and published a major report, *Mission-Shaped Church*. This looked at what was happening on the ground, gave practical help and advice, and made some recommendations for effective church planting. It has outsold every previous church report, reflecting perhaps the thirst that exists for innovative approaches to mission within the mainstream of the Church of England. Ten years earlier the Church of England had published *Breaking New Ground*, a report that had concluded that fresh expressions of church were primarily a way of supplementing 'traditional' church. By the time that *Mission-Shaped Church* was published it had become clear that it could no longer be expected that 'traditional church' would, on its own, meet the needs of the day. The parish system, together with inherited patterns of organization and worship, is still important but it cannot take on the whole task of mission as required by today's Church. The report recommends that England be regarded as a mission field and that appropriate strategies are developed, each unique to their own particular set of circumstances, to address this. It identifies five groups for whom different approaches are needed:

- regular attenders;
- fringe attenders;
- open de-churched – who have had some church connection and who may be open to returning;
- closed de-churched – who used to attend at some stage in their lives but who would not return;
- non-churched – a growing proportion of the population, consisting of those who have never had a connection with the Church, and are not seeking one.

You may well be able to think of people in your own parish who fit into these categories. What is your church doing to engage with them? Is there a role here for the Reader, either to begin to develop new initiatives, or perhaps to do something as simple and as practical as making contact with those who used to be an active part of the life of the Church but who simply seem to have disappeared off its radar? Might it be that the Reader, aware of the faces and names and detail of the local picture, could take responsibility in the Church for maintaining or re-establishing contact with those people who may simply be awaiting a personal invitation to return – not necessarily to a fresh expression, but perhaps to 'traditional' church? The Reader is often there as successive incumbents come and go and may be better placed than clergy to re-establish contact with, and nurture, those on the fringes and the open de-churched.

You can find out more by visiting: <www.cofe.anglican.org/info/papers/mission_shaped_church.pdf>. This site has the full text of the report (which can also be bought in book form). You might also like to visit <www.acpi.org.uk>, the website of the Anglican Church Planting Initiatives organization.

Fresh Expressions has made a huge impact on the Church in a relatively short space of time, nurturing, building confidence, working hard at understanding theologically this new work of God that is making its mark on the Church. Above all, although those engaged in this may be innovative (or fresh) in the way they go about things (their expression), they are preaching not something new but the same gospel interpreted for today, shown to be relevant to people's lives and expressed in a way that speaks to them in their own culture and daily living. This could be taken as implying that those who are involved in Fresh Expressions of church regard traditional church to be outmoded or irrelevant, but that isn't what this new movement is about. Traditional church has a place, it continues to speak to very many people, but many others find it difficult to access and need an approach that starts in a quite different place, where they are, not where the established worshipping community is.

So let's look briefly at the theology that underpins the Fresh Expressions movement in order that we might see where Reader ministry fits into this.

Some clear models of church have been identified that are rooted in scripture but that have not played a very big part in the Church's thinking down the centuries. George Lings[4] takes Acts 1.8 – 'But you will receive power when the Holy Spirit has come upon you; and you will be my witnesses in Jerusalem, in all Judea and Samaria, and to the ends of the earth' – and loosely maps onto this the groups identified by *Mission-Shaped Church*:

> Existing church attenders could be described as Jerusalem people. Those on the fringe are not unlike those living in Judea, who sometimes attend. The missionary journey to Judeans is justly centripetal. They would see increased commitment in terms of deeper attachment to a Jerusalem. The closed dechurched could be likened to those in Samaria, having in common an unfortunate story of distance, distrust and dislike in regard to Jerusalem . . . The non churched, and those of other world faiths, who are ignorant of the core of Christianity, or believe themselves rightly dismissive of it, can be likened to the Greeks and Romans who thought the Jews were strange, not least for their lack of idols, their insular cultural particularity and different moral stances. While Greek and Romans do not represent the ultimate ends of the earth, they were at least a yet further stage out toward it.                    (Lings, 2004)

Fresh Expressions and the 'mission-shaped' movement within the Church raise some huge and important questions for Reader ministry:

- Do Readers belong primarily 'at the centre', that is, 'in Jerusalem', or 'at the ends of the earth'?
- How can Readers bridge the two, interpreting the contemporary world to the traditional Church and finding appropriate ways of

speaking the gospel into the many spheres, cultures and contexts within which people's day-to-day lives are lived?

- Might some Readers be among the best equipped people in the Church to lead teams that investigate how the local 'mission field' can best be understood and worked in?

But there is definitely scope for some Readers to be more courageous too; only a few are currently involved in Fresh Expressions of church and fewer still have initiated one. As different ways of being church are tried, so more people are feeling confident enough to take a risk and to step out of their comfort zone into the great unknown territory of God's purpose and plans. Pause to ask yourself when your church last took a really in-depth look at its mission strategy. What happens in your parish when people seem to slide off the edge of the congregation? Is there a strategy for helping them to re-engage or do they just drift away? Are there any opportunities for doing church differently where you are? Have you had ideas beginning to take shape in your head about a new way of being church that might work in your context, but perhaps have been afraid of sharing them? Or it may be that you could get involved in a supportive role – not everything to which a Reader can productively contribute has to be initiated by the Reader him- or herself.

There is a small number of examples across the Church of England of Readers initiating ventures that reach beyond the bounds of traditional church to meet people where they are – literally in terms of place, or figuratively in terms of 'where they are spiritually'. Two of these are a 'breakfast church' in the North West and a community-based church for people in an elderly person's complex in the South. Sometimes such new ventures are planned as Fresh Expressions of church but often they simply emerge out of prayer and a real, theologically thought-out engagement with the local community and its life.

# 12

# Rules and regulations

In this chapter we shall look at the principles and practice of regulation as they touch on Reader ministry.

Every organization – including every Church – has expectations and boundaries that enable it to operate effectively and that help people to understand how its values find expression in its life and actions. We can see the principle of regulation emerging in the New Testament (a number of places in 1 Corinthians, and hints in Matthew 18.15–17, for example). Good order in the Christian community is a strong biblical principle; it complements (rather than contradicts) notions of freedom in the Spirit.

Over the centuries, the Churches of the Anglican Communion have evolved patterns of regulations, instructions, guidelines and indicators of good practice that have been adapted in response to the needs of different ages and places. Readers exercise their ministry within the Church's framework of regulation. Recognizing that principle, and living and ministering in accordance with it, is part of what it means to accept the authority of the Church.

The Church of England has a particular relationship with the state through *establishment* – in other words, there are some elements in the Church of England's governing structures and rules that are set up by the law of the land, or that have the force of law. This does not apply in quite the same way outside England.

Laws, rules and regulations affecting the ministry of Readers come from a number of sources. Reader ministry must clearly conform to the *law of the land*. This is relevant, for example, in circumstances such as child protection legislation and the implementation of new safeguarding procedures in 2009. It is not possible to say, 'We're the Church, we're special and we don't need to comply.'

*Measures* are passed by the General Synod. In England, they have the force of law once they have been approved by a committee of Parliament and have received royal assent. They cover a range of

141

subjects, from parish organization and the appointment of church-wardens to property and finance.

*Canons* are regulations passed by General Synod, which are binding particularly on lay and ordained ministers. We shall look in more detail at the Canons shortly.

*Rubrics* are the directions printed in the Book of Common Prayer and *Common Worship* and other service books. They have an important role in encouraging good practice in worship, and in discouraging idiosyncratic and unprofessional ways of leading it. It is important, especially when you begin to lead worship, that you read the rubrics carefully.

Each diocese has its own set of *Reader regulations* that set out what must, ought (and ought not) and may be done by Readers in the exercise of their ministry. They will be based on the House of Bishops' (national) Regulations for Reader ministry, adapted as necessary to local context and custom. In addition to affirming the content of the Canons that relate to Reader ministry, these diocesan regulations are likely to set out the process governing selection, training, admission and licensing, conditions of service, financial matters and grievance and disciplinary procedures, as well as including anything else that is relevant to the local situation. Sometimes the Church sets out clearly what a particular person or category of person must or must not do: some of the Canons are hard and fast and must be obeyed by all people at all times. For example, the rule that only those who are episcopally ordained priests may preside at the Eucharist (Canon B12) is absolute and applies without exception. Others are there to create a positive attitude and set out some good ideas to which people might ideally aspire: so, Canon C24 sets out principles of good practice for priests who have a responsibility for parishes ('a cure of souls'). At other times, the Church's hopes for its well-being and good ordering are set out in a more exhortatory way; they encourage and inspire and (behind the 'lawyerly' language) give a positive lead rather than prescribe a long list of musts and don'ts. An example would be Canons B43 and B44, which are there to encourage practical expression of mutual commitment with our ecumenical partners.

# Readers and Canon Law

The Canons of the Church of England can seem to be little more than a dry and dusty document and probably aren't on most people's list of essential reading, but they carry real and weighty legal status and play an important part in the good governance of the Church and its life. Those who are public ministers in the Church need to have some idea of what they are about, and Readers in particular will want to be familiar with Canons E4, E5 and E6, which relate to Reader ministry. These Canons state the nature and extent of the involvement that Readers have in the Church's public ministry, though of course they can only set out categories of engagement. 'It shall be lawful for a reader . . . generally to undertake such pastoral and educational work and to give such assistance to any minister as the bishop may direct.' This is deliberately expressed in broad and general terms because the Church at national level should not be prescribing too closely the day-to-day involvement of the Reader in his or her ministerial context. With this in mind, let's look at what the Canons say in relation to Readers. Like other legal documents, they follow the convention (archaic as this may now seem) of saying 'he' when they mean 'he or she' throughout.

Canon E4 sets out what a Reader may do:

1. A lay person, whether man or woman, who is baptized and confirmed and who satisfies the bishop that he is a regular communicant of the Church of England may be admitted by the bishop of the diocese to the office of reader in the Church and licensed by him to perform the duties which may lawfully be performed by a reader according to the provisions of paragraph 2 of this Canon or which may from time to time be so determined by Act of Synod.

2. It shall be lawful for a reader:
   (a) to visit the sick, to read and pray with them, to teach in Sunday school and elsewhere, and generally to undertake such pastoral and educational work and to give such assistance to any minister as the bishop may direct;
   (b) during the time of divine service to read Morning and Evening Prayer (save for the Absolution), to publish banns of marriage at Morning and Evening Prayer (on occasions on which a layman is permitted by the statute law so to do, and in accordance with the requirements of that law), to

read the word of God, to preach, to catechize the children, and to receive and present the offerings of the people;

(c) to distribute the holy sacrament of the Lord's Supper to the people.

2A. The bishop may also authorize a reader to bury the dead or read the burial service before, at or after a cremation but only, in each case, with the goodwill of the persons responsible and at the invitation of the minister of a parish or an extra-parochial place within the meaning of section 1 of the Deaconesses and Lay Ministry Measure 1972.

When a cure is vacant the reference in this paragraph to the minister of a parish shall be construed as a reference to the rural dean.

We might want to ask about the relevance of some of this for our own day.

- Surely anyone who is an active part of the Church can visit the sick, teach Sunday school and engage in pastoral and educational work?
- A range of people lead Morning and Evening Prayer, often following a course of training that comprises just a few hours spread over a number of weeks; others teach children, read in church and receive the collection.
- It is more common nowadays for a Reader to take funerals and although by law anyone can take a funeral, only those authorized by the Church of England may do so in its name. In other words, if a service is claimed to be an Anglican funeral, whether in church or at a crematorium, it must be conducted by someone who has been trained and approved by the Church to do so. There are people here and there who have set themselves up in business as experts in leading funerals outside of the church structures, but whenever they use words and prayers that form part of the official prayer books of the Church of England, whether the Book of Common Prayer or *Common Worship*, they do so outside the approved and authorized structures of the Church.
- Although it is only since 1988 that Readers have been authorized to distribute Holy Communion on account of holding the bishop's licence to minister, and without needing any additional approval, this was really only a tidying up of what very often happened anyway. The Canons now say that it 'shall be lawful'

for a Reader to distribute Holy Communion – but of course an incumbent can seek the bishop's permission to allow other lay people to do this too. Readers are sometimes authorized to conduct services of Public Worship with Holy Communion by Extension (sometimes called 'Extended Communion'), but that permission is not generally included within the normal Reader's licence. The House of Bishops has published special guidelines on Communion by Extension: see <www.cofe.anglican.org/worship/liturgy/commonworship/texts/other/extension/extensionend.html>.

There is very little, then, that a Reader can do that cannot also be done by others, sometimes with very little training. This can lead to a sense of unease that Reader ministry is not in itself 'unique'. This is a slight misunderstanding. As we have seen, there is no 'one thing' that makes Reader ministry unique; instead it is a gathering together of a range of features including function (e.g. preaching, teaching, etc.) and identity (lay people often with extensive experience of work in secular employment). What is distinctive about Reader ministry is the 'package' of aspects of ministry that a Reader can engage with – it is the particular constellation of training and skills and experience that makes Reader ministry unique, rather than any one specific part of it. The Canons regularize this, the Church recognizes it in many ways, not least in its public services of licensing to this public ministry, services that in many dioceses are held in the cathedral. This is the Church giving a great big stamp of approval as it launches people into the world to minister in Christ's name on behalf of the gospel and the Church.

Before someone can reach this stage and be admitted to the office of Reader and licensed to a particular sphere of ministry, Canon Law states that they must be supported by the minister of the parish or district to which they belong, and that the bishop must be assured of the suitability of the candidate. They must make the 'Declaration of Assent', which follows a preface read aloud by the bishop or his commissary (someone appointed by the bishop to act in his place and with his authority):

The Church of England is part of the One, Holy, Catholic and Apostolic Church, worshipping the one true God, Father, Son and Holy Spirit. It professes the faith uniquely revealed in the Holy Scriptures and set forth in the catholic creeds, which faith the Church is called upon to proclaim afresh in each generation. Led by the Holy Spirit, it has borne witness to Christian truth in its historic formularies, the Thirty-nine Articles of Religion, The Book of Common Prayer and the Ordering of Bishops, Priests and Deacons. In the declaration you are about to make, will you affirm your loyalty to this inheritance of faith as your inspiration and guidance under God in bringing the grace and truth of Christ to this generation and making Him known to those in your care?

I, *A B*, do so affirm, and accordingly declare my belief in the faith which is revealed in the Holy Scriptures and set forth in the catholic creeds and to which the historic formularies of the Church of England bear witness; and in public prayer I will use only the forms of service which are authorized or allowed by Canon. I, *A B*, will give due obedience to the Lord Bishop of *C* and his successors in all things lawful and honest.

The Declaration is important because:

- It roots Anglicans firmly within the Christian story, affirming that our faith is that revealed by scripture and set out in the creeds of the Church.
- It acknowledges that the ways in which the Church of England framed and defined itself in those early years in which it worked out its identity are an authentic part of this Christian story. Where we have come from plays an important part in understanding where we are now and where we are going.
- It commits people
  - to a ministry that is accountable;
  - to using authorized forms of worship (though where there is no prescribed form it is permitted to create worship that is consistent with the Church's teaching);
  - to recognizing the authority of the bishop, the chief minister who exercises episcope or oversight within and on behalf of the Church.

Canon E5.5 says: 'The bishop shall admit a person to the office of reader by the delivery of the New Testament, but without the imposition of hands.' Candidates are admitted to the office of Reader with prayer but without hands being laid on them (distinguishing it from the action used at ordination) and immediately after this they are given a New Testament – the word of God that they now have a special responsibility to proclaim. Once someone has been made a Reader they are not re-admitted to the office if they move to a different diocese, though they would, of course, need a new licence to undertake new work in a new place. Which brings us onto the subject of licensing. Canon E5 rather assumes that this will also be the place in which they will eventually minister as Readers, but the situation has changed on the ground and Reader trainees are now advised in many dioceses that they may be asked to serve elsewhere following their licensing. If Readers are to be regarded as a resource and as major contributors to the Church's ministry, we can see that it makes sense for them to be deployable to some extent, while taking account of course of their personal circumstances and needs.

We noted earlier that people must be authorized to exercise their ministry and this takes the form of a licence, issued by the diocesan bishop. The licence is only given after the Reader has made the Declaration of Assent (which is reaffirmed each time a Reader – or any other authorized minister – takes up a new role in the Church) and made a declaration of canonical obedience to the diocesan bishop. They must also make and sign this declaration (omitting the reference to the bishop if a separate declaration of obedience has just been taken, for example at an admission service):

> I, *A B*, about to be licensed to exercise the office of reader in the parish (or diocese) of *C*, do hereby promise to endeavour, as far as in me lies, to promote peace and unity, and to conduct myself as becomes a worker for Christ, for the good of his Church, and for the spiritual welfare of all people. I will give due obedience to the Bishop of *C* and his successors and the minister in whose cure I may serve, in all things lawful and honest.

This declaration is a statement that the Reader will work for the good of the gospel and the Church and will behave in a way that is appropriate for someone to whom the Church is entrusting its public ministry. It also commits the Reader to working with the incumbent of the parish. This does not mean that the vicar is free to 'lord it over' the rest of the ministry team; he or she will also have taken the oath of obedience to the bishop and all are called to work together that the gospel may be heard.

The important thing in all of this is that Readers don't simply see themselves as being the 'bottom rung' of the ministerial ladder or 'the vicar's helper' but as those lay people in whom the Church vests significant responsibility for its ministry, in the Church, in the world, and all in the name of Christ.

The complete Canons of the Church of England can be bought in printed form or they can be downloaded at <www. cofe.anglican.org/about/churchlawlegis/canons/complete.pdf>. Those directly about Reader ministry can be found at <www.cofe. anglican.org/about/churchlawlegis/canons/lay.pdf>.

# 13

# And so to conclude . . .

In *Reader Ministry Explored* we have reviewed the ways in which Reader ministry both came into being and is exercised in the Church today. We have also seen just how diverse are the roles that Readers undertake. The many stories of Readers in the Church of England today illustrate clearly that this particular form of public, authorized ministry cannot be closely and tightly defined. God calls all sorts of people to exercise the ministry of Reader, doing whatever it is that the Church needs to be done by theologically competent lay people. We have identified and discussed some of the questions that are around in the Church at the present time with regard to the purpose and distinctiveness of the Reader role but we have not attempted to give set answers to the questions that people are asking. If we are sure of one thing, it is that such an approach must always ultimately be unsatisfactory, for when the next difficult question comes along it simply means that another ready-made answer has to be sought. What we have attempted to do instead is engage you in the 'doing of the theology' involved, making suggestions as to how this process of theological reflection might be tackled by those seeking, training for, or engaged in, this ministry.

Being able to minister as a Reader depends on motive, means and opportunity (though there the similarity with a whodunnit ends!).

- The *motive* is on the same lines as the marks of mission – to tell and show what it means to live life inspired by Christ, to care for others in his name, to build a just society and to be good stewards of resources.
- The *means* are what God gives us – our own gifts and abilities, which are part of a mosaic of gifts, a pattern of many different shaped and coloured pieces. Gifts are given in order to be exercised within a context of mutual respect and interdependence (Rom.

12.3–8; 1 Cor. 12), putting to good use both the inherited and innovative mission resources of the whole Church. Responding to God's call as actual or potential ministers means exploring what God intends us to be and to do. It means joining the adventure of building up our own and others' gifts so that they can flourish – and that building up includes a lifetime of learning, creative reflection and new initiative.

- The *opportunity* is every encounter that we have, every decision that we make, and every attitude we form. For public ministers, many of those encounters and decisions sit not simply in the capacity of some private individual, but as a representative. In other words, a minister is someone who both represents the Church and the Christian faith corporately to the world at large, and who also has a leadership role in helping to shape the internal dynamics of the Church according to the ways of Christ (Col. 3.12–17). At the point where we meet anyone, we bear the responsibility of portraying to that person whether faith is worthwhile (that is, whether it really is life-changing and liberating to respond to Christ's invitation to build a relationship with him): 'I became [the Church's] servant according to God's commission that was given to me for you, to make the word of God fully known' (Col. 1.25).

One of the greatest features of Reader ministry is that it is dynamic. Its origins can be found in a response to a particular need in the Victorian era and it has continued to respond to the needs of world and Church ever since. Part of the complexity involved in defining Reader ministry is that it is by its nature responsive, shifting and changing according to the needs it meets; thus a Reader in one context may look relatively different from a Reader in another context. This is the challenge of Reader ministry – and, as with many challenges, it is exhilarating, frustrating, inspiring, frightening, exciting and daunting. It is in fact the fluidity of Reader ministry that makes it such a gift to the Church, as generation after generation of lay people are called out to learn the craft of 'reading between the lines' of scripture and theology, context and culture, Church and world and to proclaim this in word and deed in all that they do.

# Appendix 1
# Reader ministry and ordination

Although it is not the principal focus of this book, it is worth us taking a very brief look here at ordained ministry and exploring, in particular, the relationship between deacon and Reader. The Church of England, in common with other churches, retains the three historic orders of bishop (overseer), priest (presbyter, or elder) and deacon (one who serves the church community). All those ordained are ordained initially to the office and work of a deacon in the Church. It is essential, therefore, that all those whom the Church ordains have a servant heart; they must 'serve a title' as a curate in a parish for three or four years, either full-time or alongside their work or other daily activity. The Ordinal published as part of *Common Worship* says of deacons:

> Deacons are ordained so that the people of God may be better equipped to make Christ known. Theirs is a life of visible self-giving. Christ is the pattern of their calling and their commission; as he washed the feet of his disciples, so they must wash the feet of others.
>
> (*Common Worship Ordination Services*, 2007, p. 10)

A few people remain as deacons – it is their specific calling – but for most it forms the first year in orders at the end of which they are ordained priest. When ordained priest they do not stop being deacons; the servant ministry of Christ continues to lie at the heart of all that they are and all that they offer. After a curacy, many priests go on to work in parishes as vicars, rectors or priests-in-charge. Others retain their previous employment and minister within this, often in a very incarnational (Christ-present) but unsung sort of way, 'being Christ' in all sorts of circumstances and among all sorts of people. In order to minister on behalf of the Church of England they must still be licensed, either to a parish or perhaps to a hospital, prison or educational chaplaincy. The Church calls a very small number of ordained people to serve as bishops. They will be overseers of a diocese, or will work as a suffragan bishop with a diocesan bishop in the work of oversight, and will carry a particular pastoral responsibility for the clergy as well as for the policies and strategies by which the gospel will be proclaimed to the people in their charge. Even if people are called and ordained to be bishops they remain both deacons and priests; the pattern of service taught and demonstrated by Jesus is to be the pattern of their calling. Many would argue that the greater the position of responsibility to which people are called, the greater awareness they need to have of their duty to serve others.

One can see that the roles of bishop and priest are distinctively different from that of the Reader, but what about the deacon? Is there enough that separates these two for the Church to continue to regard them as separate ministries? There has been ongoing debate in the Church for some years about the relationship between the ministry of the deacon, a minister in holy orders, and the Reader, who remains a lay person. The Church has addressed the question in two recent reports: *The Mission and Ministry of the Whole Church* and *Reader Upbeat.*[5]

There are three main reasons that we have chosen not to take a particular stance on this issue in *Reader Ministry Explored*:

- The detail of the debate falls outside the remit that we have set for ourselves.
- There is a wide range of opinion, with some people valuing highly the lay status of Reader ministry and others feeling that Readers could equally well – and perhaps ought to – be ordained deacon.
- This is a complex matter and one for decision by the whole Church.

# Appendix 2
# Review of ministry for Readers in the Diocese of York

You may find these notes helpful as you prepare for your review interview; please feel free to ignore the points that, because of the context of your ministry, are not of relevance to you. When [insert person] arranges your interview, you will be sent a response sheet: please return it before the interview, highlighting any aspects that you would particularly wish to discuss.

Almighty God, by whose grace alone we are accepted and called to your service: strengthen us by your Holy Spirit and make us worthy of our calling; through Jesus Christ your Son our Lord, who is alive and reigns with you, in the unity of the Holy Spirit, one God, now and for ever.

### Welcome and introduction

- I have recently found the most rewarding and enjoyable aspects of ministry to be . . . because . . .
- But aspects I have found less so are . . . because . . .

### Called to be an ambassador for Christ

- Looking back over the period leading up to this review, I have had opportunities to . . .
  - . . . participate as a leader and encourager of others in public worship . . . I would hope to see future developments in the areas of . . .
  - . . . preach and explain the Christian faith . . . I enjoy preaching about . . . but I can find it harder to engage with . . .
  - . . . serve the community through (schools, work with community groups, work outside specifically church settings, community projects and regeneration initiatives) . . . I have valued these because . . . but some of them present particular challenges . . .
  - . . . be an advocate for the Christian faith outside the specific church context . . .
- To me, being a public and representative minister has meant . . .

- People who know me would say that my particular strengths in Reader ministry are . . .
- I have had opportunities to be part of new ventures in terms of evangelism, through work with adults, children and young people, for which the most effective means have been . . .
- When I reflect on my theology and understanding of mission and outreach I sense that it has changed or developed because . . .
- The opportunities I have had for working ecumenically with others from across the spectrum of Christian traditions include . . . and I can see areas for further development in . . .

## Called to be a disciple of Christ

- Things I have learned recently from reflecting on how people develop in their faith, prayer and discipleship include . . . and this has influenced my preaching, teaching and leading of worship in so far as . . .
- I have had opportunities to help others to be supported in their Christian discipleship in daily life, such as . . .
- I have had both enriching and demanding pastoral situations recently, such as . . . They have led me to think afresh about . . .
- I recognize that my own understanding of faith has changed, in that I would now say or ask . . . I would like to follow this up through study, in which case I would welcome help or guidance in . . .
- My experience of working at sustaining a life of disciplined study and reflection has been . . . I have got some new insights or issues that have emerged from this, for example . . .
- I have been able to take part in continuing ministerial education . . . and would welcome opportunities or guidance in the area of . . .
- My opportunities for developing and sustaining contacts with those of other world faiths have been . . . and my reflections are . . .

## Called to celebrate the gifts of Christ to his people

- During the period leading up to this review, these are the reflections that I would have on . . .
  - . . . building up collaboration in Christian witness and ministry
  - . . . seeing change take place, and facilitating it where appropriate
  - . . . ministering alongside others

## Called to care for the household of faith, and to reflect the life of Christ in our own life

- My experience of being called to lead a life of personal prayer has been . . . My sense of being sustained in the pressures and joys of serving Christ has been . . .

- My experience of finding opportunity for worship that helps me to grow and to be fed spiritually has been . . .
- I have had opportunities to reflect with others about my continuing development as a leader, a person of prayer and as a pastor, such as . . .
- My reflections about the management of the various calls on my time and attention, including those that are associated with ministry, are . . .
- [In terms of what I see as my family] I have been able to offer sufficient support to my family particularly in respect of . . . while I would welcome a greater opportunity in respect of . . .

## Please add any other issues which you wish to raise on the response sheet

*Thank you for participating in Review of Ministry*

You may like to take a look at the Church of England Readers' Website, and especially at the resources page: <www.readers.cofe.anglican.org>.

# Notes

1 In a recent Church of England report it was suggested that, given the difficulty of the name 'Reader', that Readers should be called 'Lay ministers (Reader)'. This has not yet caught on in many dioceses so we have decided to use the title 'Reader' as this will be more familiar for most readers of the book.

2 The Clergy of the Church of England Database (CCEd) is a collaborative project, funded by the Arts and Humanities Research Council and bringing together scholars from King's College London, the University of Kent at Canterbury and the University of Reading. Its objective is to create a relational database documenting the careers of all Church of England clergymen between 1540 and 1835.

3 This is classically described by G. Gibbs, *Learning by Doing: A Guide to Teaching and Learning Methods*, Oxford, Further Education Unit, Oxford Polytechnic (now Oxford Brookes University), 1988.

4 George Lings is Director of the Sheffield Centre, which was established in 1991 to be a centre of excellence in church planting and evangelism.

5 GS Misc 854 (2007) and GS 1689 (2008), published by the General Synod of the Church of England, available from Church House Bookshop, London SW1P 3BN.

# References and further reading

## Introduction

*The Canons of the Church of England* (2008), 6th edn, London, Church House Publishing. Also available as a free download from the Church of England's website <www.cofe.org.uk>.

Kuhrt, G. and Nappin, P. (eds) (2002), *Bridging the Gap: Reader Ministry Today*, London, Church House Publishing.

## 1 Public ministry as a part of the ministry of the whole people of God

Dearborn, T. (1998), *Beyond Duty: A Passion for Christ, a Heart for Mission*, London, MARC.

Kuhrt, G. and Nappin, P. (eds) (2002), *Bridging the Gap: Reader Ministry Today*, London, Church House Publishing.

## 2 Tracing the history of Reader ministry

*The Chronicles of the Convocation of Canterbury for 1859* (1859), London, E. Thompson.

*The Chronicles of the Convocation of Canterbury for 1844* (1844), London, E. Thompson.

Hiscox, R. (1991), *Celebrating Reader Ministry: 125 Years of Lay Ministry in the Church of England*, London, Mowbray.

King, T. G. (1973), *Readers: A Pioneer Minstry*, London, Central Readers' Board.

Martineau, R. (1970), *The Office and Work of a Reader*, Oxford, Mowbray.

Thorpe, W. (2003), *Equipping the Saints*, London, Church House Publishing.

*York Journal of Convocation 1889* (1889), London, E. Thompson.

## 5 Formal study

Buzan, T. (2006), *The Buzan Study Skills Handbook: The Shortcut to Success in Your Studies with Mind Mapping, Speed Reading and Winning Memory Techniques*, London, BBC Active.

Cottrell, S. (2008), *The Study Skills Handbook*, 3rd edn, Basingstoke, Palgrave Macmillan.

Northedge, A. (2005), *The Good Study Guide*, 2nd edn, Milton Keynes, Open University Worldwide.

*Shaping the Future: New Patterns of Training for Lay and Ordained* (2006), London, Church House Publishing.

## 6 Developing practical skills

*Common Worship: Services and Prayers for the Church of England* (2000), London, Church House Publishing.

Day, D. (2004), *A Preaching Workbook*, new edn, London, SPCK.

Eliot, T. S. (2001), *Four Quartets*, London, Faber and Faber.

*Guidelines for the Professional Conduct of the Clergy* (2003), London, Church House Publishing.

Honey, P. and Mumford, A. (2006), *Learning Styles Questionnaire 2006: 80 Item Version*, Maidenhead, Peter Honey Publications.

Stevenson, G. and Wright, S. (2008), *Preaching with Humanity: A Practical Guide for Today's Church*, London, Church House Publishing.

## 11 Fresh Expressions of church and Reader ministry

*Breaking New Ground: Church Planting in the Church of England* (1994), London, Church House Publishing.

Lings, G. (2008), 'The Jerusalem Trap', available at <www.encountersontheedge.org.uk/main/Reports/canada08/Jerusalem.htm>.

*Mission-Shaped Church: Church Planting and Fresh Expressions of Church in a Changing Context* (2004), London, Church House Publishing.

## Appendix 1: Reader ministry and ordination

*Common Worship: Ordination Services (Study Edition)* (2007), London, Church House Publishing.